AF334632

African Political, Economic, and Security Issues

Humanitarian Crisis and Response in the Horn of Africa

African Political, Economic, and Security Issues

Additional books in this series can be found on Nova's website
under the Series tab.

Additional E-books in this series can be found on Nova's website
under the E-book tab.

AFRICAN POLITICAL, ECONOMIC, AND SECURITY ISSUES

HUMANITARIAN CRISIS AND RESPONSE IN THE HORN OF AFRICA

CHARLEY J. NEWSOME

AND

HELLEN I. HERRON

EDITORS

Nova Science Publishers, Inc.

New York

Copyright © 2012 by Nova Science Publishers, Inc.

All rights reserved. No part of this book may be reproduced, stored in a retrieval system or transmitted in any form or by any means: electronic, electrostatic, magnetic, tape, mechanical photocopying, recording or otherwise without the written permission of the Publisher.

For permission to use material from this book please contact us:
Telephone 631-231-7269; Fax 631-231-8175
Web Site: http://www.novapublishers.com

NOTICE TO THE READER

The Publisher has taken reasonable care in the preparation of this book, but makes no expressed or implied warranty of any kind and assumes no responsibility for any errors or omissions. No liability is assumed for incidental or consequential damages in connection with or arising out of information contained in this book. The Publisher shall not be liable for any special, consequential, or exemplary damages resulting, in whole or in part, from the readers' use of, or reliance upon, this material. Any parts of this book based on government reports are so indicated and copyright is claimed for those parts to the extent applicable to compilations of such works.

Independent verification should be sought for any data, advice or recommendations contained in this book. In addition, no responsibility is assumed by the publisher for any injury and/or damage to persons or property arising from any methods, products, instructions, ideas or otherwise contained in this publication.

This publication is designed to provide accurate and authoritative information with regard to the subject matter covered herein. It is sold with the clear understanding that the Publisher is not engaged in rendering legal or any other professional services. If legal or any other expert assistance is required, the services of a competent person should be sought. FROM A DECLARATION OF PARTICIPANTS JOINTLY ADOPTED BY A COMMITTEE OF THE AMERICAN BAR ASSOCIATION AND A COMMITTEE OF PUBLISHERS.

Additional color graphics may be available in the e-book version of this book.

Library of Congress Cataloging-in-Publication Data

ISBN: 978-1-61942-540-8

Published by Nova Science Publishers, Inc. + New York

CONTENTS

PREFACE

As a result of the worst drought in 60 years, regional conflicts, and conflict within states, a humanitarian emergency of massive proportion is unfolding in the Horn of Africa region with more than 13.3 million people affected, 750,000 of whom need food assistance in the near future to avoid death. Somalia has been hardest hit so far, creating population displacement within its borders and a refugee crisis of nearly 1 million people in the region, primarily in Kenya and Ethiopia. The international community is responding, and the humanitarian needs are expected to rise and will likely demand sustained attention. This book provides an overview of the current status of the crisis, a summary of the background on the region, a framework for the international and humanitarian response, and an analysis of some of the operational challenges.

Chapter 1 - As a result of the worst drought in 60 years, regional conflicts, and conflict within states, a humanitarian emergency of massive proportion is unfolding in the Horn of Africa region with more than 13.3 million people affected, 750,000 of whom need food assistance in the near term to avoid death. Somalia has been hardest hit so far, creating population displacement within its borders and a refugee crisis of nearly 1 million people in the region, primarily in Kenya and Ethiopia.

The international community is responding, and the humanitarian needs are expected to rise in the coming months and will likely demand sustained attention well into 2012. While life-saving assistance is the current priority, long-term responses may be needed to break the disaster cycle in the Horn. Though triggered by drought, the humanitarian emergency is further complicated by political and security pressures within, between, and among the various countries in the region. This report provides an overview of the current status of the crisis, a summary of the background on the region, a framework for the international and humanitarian response, and an analysis of some of the operational challenges.

Chapter 2 - Chairman Coons, Ranking Member Isakson, and distinguished members of the Committee, thank you for this opportunity to testify before you today on the humanitarian crisis in the Horn of Africa. Your attention and concern is critical, as the situation continues to deteriorate daily, with millions of individuals affected.

In scale and severity, the current drought in the Horn of Africa is the worst in 60 years and, according to the UN Office of the Coordination for Humanitarian Affairs, it is now affecting an estimated 12.4 million people in Somalia, Kenya, Ethiopia, and Djibouti. It is both a humanitarian and a security crisis, as famine has been declared in the difficult to access areas of Somalia and refugees are pouring across the borders into already drought-stressed areas of Kenya and Ethiopia.

I will discuss today the current situation, our immediate response, the challenges we face, and our long term plans to address the chronic food insecurity in the Horn of Africa.

Chapter 3 - Good morning, Chairman Coons, Ranking Member Isakson, and members of the Committee. Thank you for holding this hearing on the drought and famine in the Horn of Africa. We share your grave concern about the ongoing humanitarian crisis in the Horn of Africa. The eastern Horn of Africa is currently experiencing one of the worst droughts since the 1950s. More than 12 million people—mainly in Ethiopia, Kenya, and Somalia—are severely affected and in need of humanitarian assistance. In Somalia, drought conditions have exacerbated a complex emergency that has continued since 1991. The information coming out of the Horn of Africa, especially the dire situation of refugees from Somalia, is devastating. In cooperation with our international and regional partners, we will continue to work to address this humanitarian crisis while continuing to support long-term political and food security in the region.

Chapter 4 - I travelled to Ethiopia and Kenya in July to evaluate the emerging refugee crisis in the region where hundreds of thousands of Somalis have fled drought and famine in Somalia. During my trip, I visited refugee camps in each country along with representatives from donor countries, met with senior government officials, talked with officials from UN agencies and nongovernmental organizations, and spoke with refugees. It was clear that this is developing into the worst humanitarian emergency that the region has seen in a generation, at least since the great famine of 1991-1992. We now must confront a refugee emergency within a protracted refugee situation. Years of hard work by the host governments and their international partners to address just the basic needs within established camps quickly are being overshadowed by the need to add new border-crossing facilities, new camps, and emergency services.

Chapter 5 - Thank you for inviting me to testify before the Sub-Committee today on the critically important issue of drought and famine in the Horn of Africa. I am here today in my capacity as Director of Policy and Advocacy for Mercy Corps, a global relief and development organization that responds to disasters and supports community development in more than forty countries around the world. Mercy Corps has worked in the Horn for many years, and we currently manage relief and development programs in the three countries most affected by the drought: Kenya, Ethiopia, and Somalia. In these countries we have hundreds of staff providing assistance to 900,000 drought victims. We are working in many of the areas most affected by the drought: North and Central Somalia, Eastern Ethiopia, and Northeastern Kenya. In these regions we are pursuing a range of drought-focused interventions, including providing access to water; supporting livelihoods so that people can afford to feed themselves and protect their livestock; aiding communities to better manage the scarce water resources that they have; and providing supplemental nutrition to at-risk children and mothers. We are undertaking these programs with the generous support of public and private donors, including the important contributions of the US Agency for International Development.

Chapter 6 - I would like to thank you very much for the opportunity to testify today on the drought and famine conditions in the Horn of Africa in general and in Somalia in particular, as well as on the response of the United States and other members of the international community to this growing crisis.

As we meet, the situation especially critical—the head of the United Nations refugee agency describes it as the "worst humanitarian disaster" in the world today—with nearly half of the Somali population, some 3.7 million people, facing starvation while at least another 11 million men, women, and children across the Horn of Africa are thought to be at risk.

Chapter 7 - Somalia is one of the most inimical countries to humanitarian aid workers. The security context and the humanitarian operational environment that both local and international aid agencies face have severely restricted humanitarian activities, particularly in areas under the control of the radical Islamist group, al Shabaab. Aid organizations responded to al Shabaab's threats by limiting areas of operations or fully suspending operations in southern Somalia. The majority of the organizations that remain active in Somalia have concentrated operations in and around territory under government control in Mogadishu, territory under the control of government-aligned administrations in central Somalia, and in the semiautonomous regions in northern Somalia of Puntland and Somaliland. In the south, the withdrawal of humanitarian aid organizations has exacerbated the effect of the Horn's severe drought on the Somali people.

Chapter 8 - Mr. Chairman, Congressman Payne, and Members of the Committee, thank you for the opportunity to testify today on the humanitarian situation in East Africa and the importance of a coordinated and sustainable US strategy. Oxfam is grateful for the work this committee has done to address the humanitarian situation affecting 12 million people today living in Ethiopia, Kenya and Somalia. We are also grateful for the leadership role the US government has played as the most generous donor, providing $600 million since the beginning of the year. Oxfam America is an international development and relief agency committed to developing lasting solutions to poverty, hunger and social injustice. We are part of a confederation of 15 Oxfam organizations working together in more than 100 countries with over 3,000 local partners around the globe.

In my testimony today, I will be outlining the humanitarian crisis in the region and providing recommendations for the US government's response based on the situation on the ground.

Chapter 9 - Somalia is located on the east coast of Africa and north of the Equator and, with Ethiopia, Eritrea, Djibouti, and Kenya, is often referred to as the Horn of Africa. It comprises Italy's former Trust Territory of Somalia and the former British Protectorate of Somaliland (now seeking recognition as an independent state). The coastline extends 2,720 kilometers (1,700 mi.).

The northern part of the country is hilly, and in many places the altitude ranges between 900 and 2,100 meters (3,000-7,000 ft.) above sea level. The central and southern areas are flat, with an average altitude of less than 180 meters (600 ft.). The Juba and the Shabelle Rivers rise in Ethiopia and flow south across the country toward the Indian Ocean. The Shabelle does not reach the sea.

Chapter 10 - Kenya has a very diverse population that includes three of Africa's major sociolinguistic groups: Bantu (67%), Nilotic (30%), and Cushitic (3%). Kenyans are deeply religious. About 80% of Kenyans are Christian, 11% Muslim, and the remainder follow traditional African religions or other faiths. Most city residents retain links with their rural, extended families and leave the city periodically to help work on the family farm. About 75% of the work force is engaged in agriculture, mainly as subsistence farmers. The national motto of Kenya is *Harambee,* meaning "pull together." In that spirit, volunteers in hundreds of communities build schools, clinics, and other facilities each year and collect funds to send students abroad.

Chapter 11 - Ethiopia is located in the Horn of Africa and is bordered on the north and northeast by Eritrea, on the east by Djibouti and Somalia, on the south by Kenya, and on the west and southwest by Sudan. The country has a high central plateau that varies from 1,800 to 3,000 meters (6,000 ft.-10,000 ft.) above sea level, with some mountains reaching 4,620 meters (15,158 ft.). Elevation is generally highest just before the point of descent to the Great Rift Valley, which splits the plateau diagonally. A number of rivers cross the plateau--notably the Blue Nile flowing from Lake Tana. The plateau gradually slopes to the lowlands of the Sudan on the west and the Somali-inhabited plains to the southeast.

Chapter 12 - Eritrea is located in the Horn of Africa and is bordered on the northeast and east by the Red Sea, on the west and northwest by Sudan, on the south by Ethiopia, and on the southeast by Djibouti. The country has a high central plateau that varies from 1,800 to 3,000 meters (6,000-10,000 ft.) above sea level. A coastal plain, western lowlands, and some 300 islands comprise the remainder of Eritrea's landmass. Eritrea has no year-round rivers.

The climate is temperate in the mountains and hot in the lowlands. Asmara, the capital, is about 2,300 meters (7,500 ft.) above sea level. Maximum temperature is 26° C (80° F). The weather is usually sunny and dry, with the short or belg rains occurring February-April and the big or meher rains beginning in late June and ending in mid-September.

Chapter 13 - About two-thirds of the Republic of Djibouti's inhabitants live in the capital city. The indigenous population is divided between the majority Somalis (predominantly of the Issa tribe, with minority Issaq and Gadabursi representation) and the Afars (Danakils). All are Cushitic-speaking peoples, and nearly all are Muslim. Among the 15,000 foreigners residing in Djibouti, the French are the most numerous. Among the French are approximately 3,000 troops.

In: Humanitarian Crisis and Response ...   ISBN: 978-1-61942-540-8
Editors: C.J. Newsome and H.I. Herron © 2012 Nova Science Publishers, Inc.

Chapter 1

HORN OF AFRICA: THE HUMANITARIAN CRISIS AND INTERNATIONAL RESPONSE

Rhoda Margesson, Ted Dagne,
Charles E. Hanrahan, Lauren Ploch,
Dianne E. Rennack, Marjorie Ann Browne
and Susan G. Chesser

SUMMARY

As a result of the worst drought in 60 years, regional conflicts, and conflict within states, a humanitarian emergency of massive proportion is unfolding in the Horn of Africa region with more than 13.3 million people affected, 750,000 of whom need food assistance in the near term to avoid death. Somalia has been hardest hit so far, creating population displacement within its borders and a refugee crisis of nearly 1 million people in the region, primarily in Kenya and Ethiopia.

The international community is responding, and the humanitarian needs are expected to rise in the coming months and will likely demand sustained attention well into 2012. While life-saving assistance is the current priority, long-term responses may be needed to break the disaster cycle in the Horn. Though triggered by drought, the humanitarian emergency is further complicated by political and security pressures within, between, and among the various countries in the region. This report provides an overview of the current status of the crisis, a summary of the background on the region, a framework for the international and humanitarian response, and an analysis of some of the operational challenges.

The role of the 112th Congress, which has so far focused on the crisis in hearings, legislation, and congressional correspondence with the Administration, is also examined, particularly with regard to funding questions, including:

- budget priorities on global humanitarian accounts and food aid;
- diversion of food aid;
- donor restrictions on aid; and
- burdensharing and donor fatigue.

It is anticipated Congress will continue to follow and respond to events as they unfold in the Horn.

INTRODUCTION

The Horn of Africa region, which includes Djibouti, Eritrea, Ethiopia, Kenya, and Somalia, is facing its worst drought in 60 years. The situation is critical with more than 13.3 million people affected, 4 million in acute need of humanitarian assistance, and 750,000 who are thought to be in dire need of food to prevent death. Conditions in Somalia have created an escalating refugee crisis, primarily in Kenya and Ethiopia. Despite considerable efforts by the United States and the international community to respond to the emergency, the needs of those affected are expected to increase in the coming months and may not stabilize until 2012. Key priorities include food, water and sanitation, health, and protection.

The United States is the largest bilateral donor of humanitarian assistance to the region, having provided over $600 million in life-saving assistance. It is also working on long-term responses to break the disaster cycle in the Horn. The urgency and scope of the humanitarian emergency, coupled with other contributing factors, such as poor infrastructure, insecurity, and internal unrest, have begun to command the attention of the international community. The 112th Congress has so far focused on the crisis in hearings, legislation, and congressional correspondence with the Administration. It is anticipated Congress will continue to follow and respond to events as they unfold in the Horn.

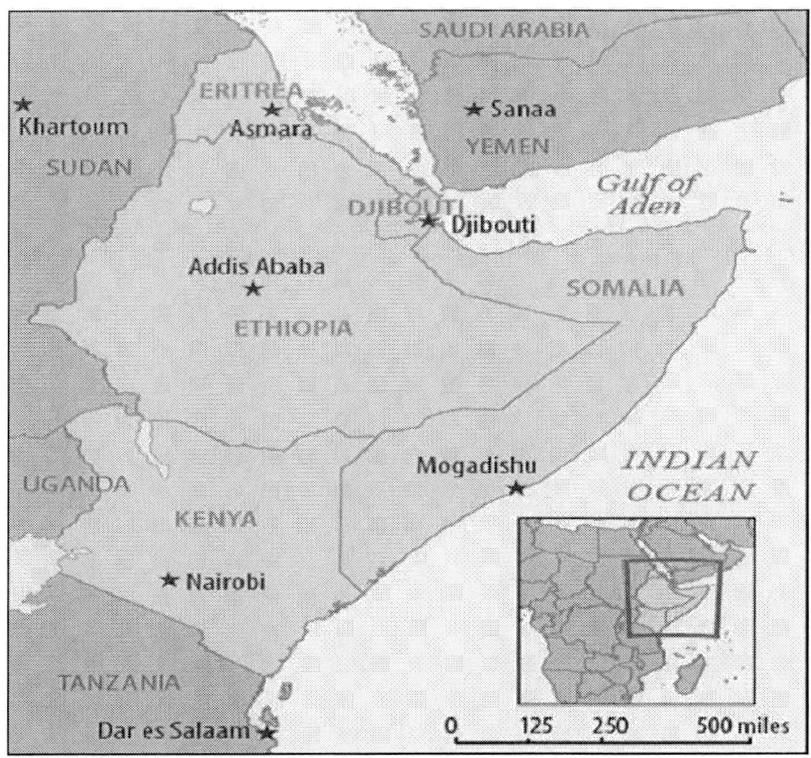

Source: Congressional Research Service.

Figure 1. Horn of Africa.

CURRENT STATUS OF THE CRISIS

On July 20, 2011, Mark Bowden, the United Nations Humanitarian Coordinator for Somalia, issued a famine declaration for two regions of southern Somalia.[1] The United Nations identified three additional areas in southern Somalia in early August and another in early September.[2] Also on July 20, the U.N. Office for the Coordination of Humanitarian Assistance (UNOCHA) elevated the status of the Horn of Africa drought crisis to a major, large-scale emergency, which brought internal resources and focus to bear within UNOCHA, such as surge capacity and additional staff.

Preliminary Numbers at a Glance

UNOCHA estimates the number of people in need of assistance, including refugees, is 13.3 million. Most are considered by the humanitarian community to be extraordinarily vulnerable, and UNOCHA has said that 750,000 are at risk of death from starvation if they do not receive assistance in the next four months. The number of deaths attributed to the crisis to date is unknown but thought to be in the tens of thousands and possibly higher.[3] It is expected to increase substantially as the crisis unfolds. Hundreds of people are dying every day due to the famine and at least half are thought to be children. The United Nations Children's Fund (UNICEF) has estimated one child is dying every six minutes in this crisis.

People Requiring Assistance by Country
(Total 13.3 million)

Kenya: 4.3 million
Ethiopia: 4.8 million
Somalia: 4.0 million
Djibouti: 165,642

(NOTE: These figures include refugees, except recent arrivals from Sudan into Ethiopia. Figures for Eritrea are unavailable.)

Number of Displaced Somalis in the Region
(Total 2.4 million)

Somali refugees in Kenya: 491,000
Somali refugees in Ethiopia: 182,000
Somali refugees in Djibouti: 18,000
Somali refugees in Yemen: 195,000
Somali Internally Displaced Persons (IDPs) (in Somalia): 1.5 million

---

Source: UNOCHA, Horn of Africa Crisis, Situation Report No. 13, September 8, 2011.
Note: Somalis have also sought refuge in smaller numbers in Uganda, Eritrea, and Tanzania.

Food Situation

The drought, compounded by conflict, has led to crop failures, loss of livelihoods (especially among livestock herders), population displacement and famine in southern and central Somalia. The U.S. Agency for International Development's (USAID's) Famine Early Warning System (FEWS NET) reports that rains were late and erratic in March through May 2011 and that rainfall totals were less than 30% of average in some areas and 60% below normal precipitation levels in northern Kenya and southern Somalia.

As crops have failed and livestock have died, food prices have soared. Extraordinarily high food and fuel prices have been reported across the region. Staple food prices (from June 2010 to June 2011) have risen by 240% in Somalia, 100% in Ethiopia, and 51% in Kenya. Diesel prices have risen by 45% in Somalia and 30% in Kenya. Critical services such as transport, access to health facilities, food distribution, and water trucking have been affected by the increase in fuel prices. UNOCHA reports that high levels of malnutrition are widespread in northern and eastern Kenya, southern Ethiopia, and central and southern Somalia. (See food shortage map below.) Poor families are unable to purchase food or fuel, contributing to the hundreds of thousands of Somalis who have moved internally or across borders in pursuit of such resources.

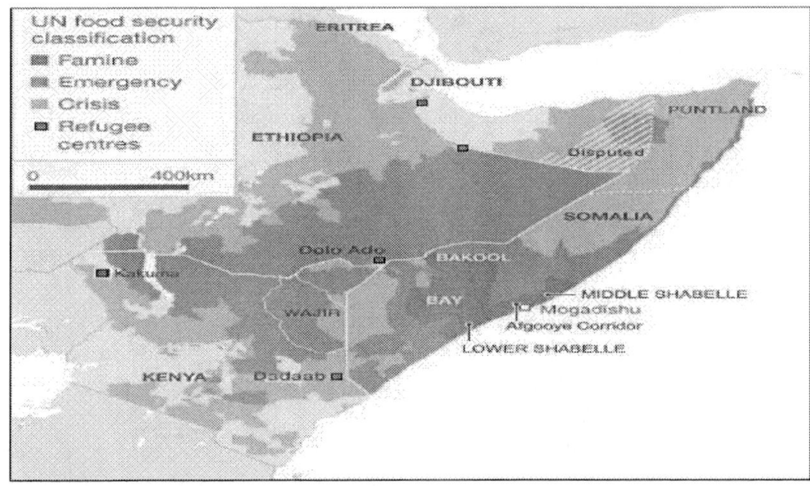

Source: BBC, August 2011, edited by CRS.

Figure 2. Food Shortage Map.

The United Nations has stated that the October to December rainfall in the most drought-affected areas of Ethiopia, Kenya, and Somalia is expected to be below average. In addition, a below-average November to January rainfall is expected in southern Somalia. The outlook for the region is that food insecurity will persist into 2012, particularly in southern Somalia, with populations not recovering until the August harvest.[4]

FEWS NET has analyzed projected food assistance needs six months into the future for three of the Horn countries where it has a staff presence: Ethiopia, Kenya, and Somalia. In Ethiopia, above average food needs are likely to persist, especially in pastoral (livestock herding) areas, although overall needs are expected to decline over the coming six months. In Kenya, three consecutive seasons of poor rainfall in the northeast indicate that food needs will be above average in January, even if forthcoming October-December rains are normal. In Somalia, famine is expected to persist into at least December. August harvests have been estimated at one-third of the 1995-2010 average, and medium-range forecasts have raised concerns about the adequacy of October-December rains. FEWS NET concludes for Somalia that "food assistance needs in February 2012 will remain far above typical levels."

Displaced Populations

Continuing insecurity and drought have had a disproportionate impact on Somalia, a country already dealing with a protracted humanitarian emergency. An Islamist insurgency led by an Al Qaeda affiliate, Al Shabaab, complicates the delivery of international aid to famine-struck areas, an issue examined in greater detail later in this report. As the effects of the drought have worsened in 2011, populations in southern Somalia have been cut off from most of the international assistance provided to other parts of the Horn of Africa. U.N. agencies warn that famine conditions may spread.[5] Many people in that part of the country are currently out of reach of most aid agencies, including the World Food Program (WFP). Dire conditions have forced many to flee their homes along what the head of WFP has called "roads of death," in search of aid at increasingly crowded refugee camps in Kenya and Ethiopia and in IDP camps in and around Mogadishu.[6]

In crises resulting from conflict or natural disasters, population movements often occur within the affected country or flow to countries in close proximity. In these situations the plight of the refugee[7] is one critical element of population movement; the internally displaced person (IDP) is another.[8] Somalia's population is estimated to be approximately 9 million. According to the U.N. High Commissioner for Refugees (UNHCR) roughly 4 million people inside Somalia are impacted by continuing insecurity and drought, of whom 3 million are in the southern regions of Somalia. This figure includes nearly 1.5 million Somali Internally Displaced Persons (IDPs).

Instability in Somalia has compounded the humanitarian situation throughout the region, as more than 918,000 Somali refugees and asylum seekers strain the limited resources of host communities, with 90% in bordering countries, including over 491,000 in Kenya, 195,000 in Yemen, 182,000 in Ethiopia, and 18,000 in Djibouti.[9]

The number of Somalis displaced by the crisis continues to change. At the end of July, Somali refugees were arriving at camps in Kenya and Ethiopia at a rate of approximately 3,300 per day (1,300 in Kenya and 2,000 in Ethiopia), many in critical condition and with children particularly susceptible to acute malnutrition. By mid-August the numbers dropped drastically in Ethiopia for reasons that are not yet fully known. By mid-September, the number of refugees arriving in Kenya had slowed to an average 1,100 per day while in Ethiopia the number ranged from approximately 350 per day to none. In Yemen, 3,700 Somalis arrived by boat during August, which was the highest reported monthly influx to the country in 2011.[10] (See map below for the location of refugee camps, transit centers, and refugee settlements.)

Kenya and Ethiopia have expressed concern about the economic, security, and demographic implications of refugees crossing their borders in large numbers. They have called for the international community to increase its efforts to deliver aid inside Somalia to avoid a pull factor across the border. The influx of refugees has strained local resources, already scarce, and in some cases caused tensions with host communities. Reports suggest that refugees are vulnerable to sexual violence and have been targeted by criminals en route to the camps and in the areas surrounding them. Kenyan officials have been accused, in some cases, of forcibly returning refugees to Somalia, a practice that would go against a key principle of the 1951 Convention Relating to the Status of Refugees and its 1967 Protocol, to which Kenya is a State Party.[11]

Health Concerns among Displaced Populations

Preventing secondary causes of death and illness related to acute malnutrition, including communicable diseases such as measles, cholera, and respiratory infections, and vector-borne diseases such as malaria, is critical. Humanitarian agencies remain very concerned about the health situation in Somalia and in the refugee camps. Communicable diseases spread more easily among vulnerable populations with poor sanitation conditions, limited safe drinking water, and overcrowded living conditions. The number of cases of measles and cholera in the refugee camps in Ethiopia and Kenya has increased dramatically. Reportedly half the measles cases among the Somali refugee population in Ethiopia are in teenagers and adults.[13] The fatality rate is high among children. Refugees arriving at the reception centers are being closely monitored. Immunization against measles in Somalia is very low and the outbreak of this disease is also affecting IDPs in Somalia, along with other diseases such as acute watery diarrhea. With the onset of the rainy season, and in some areas where flooding is anticipated if the rainfall exceeds the ground's capacity for absorption, the risk of the spread of disease is also increased.

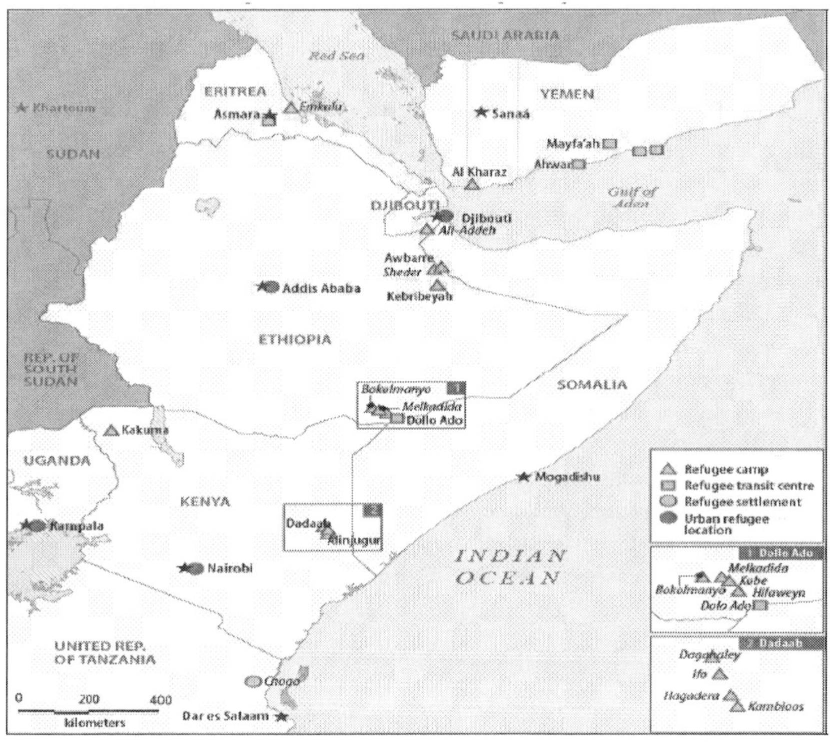

Figure 3. Horn of Africa: Refugee Map.

> **Refugee Camps in Kenya and Ethiopia: Dadaab and Dollo Ado**
>
> Kenya's Dadaab refugee complex is the largest refugee compound in the world. Established 20 years ago, some refugee families have lived in Dadaab for two decades, and there are over 6,000 third generation refugees whose parents have never been to their home countries. Dadaab hosts the largest number of registered Somali refugees in Kenya. Today, with almost half a million people, Dadaab has become the country's fourth-largest population center. In recent months, new arrivals from Somalia have spontaneously settled on the outskirts of the overcrowded Dadaab camps, from where UNHCR is attempting to assist them. Three new sites at Dadaab were opened in August 2011, and UNHCR expects to transfer up to 180,000 refugees to these new sites by the end of November. Kenya's capital, Nairobi, and a second refugee complex in Kenya, Kakuma, which is located near the South Sudan border, also host tens of thousands of Somali refugees. A smaller refugee complex in southern Ethiopia, Dollo Ado, has tripled in size in 2011.[12]

BACKGROUND ON THE REGION

In recent decades, humanitarian crises in the Horn of Africa have been caused not only by natural disasters, such as drought and famine, but also by conflict, often in the form of violent internal political turmoil and wars between and among states in the region. Much of this violence has been fueled by poor governance, corruption, and economic mismanagement.[14] Borders throughout the region remain in dispute, with small arms available in abundance, further contributing to regional and localized insecurity. The Horn has also been highly vulnerable to terrorist attacks, and currently parts of Somalia are considered a safe haven for international terrorist groups. With the exception of Kenya, the countries of the Horn rank "not free" on Freedom House's Freedom in the World 2011 survey.[15]

All these factors add to the development challenges facing the region. The countries in the Horn are among the world's poorest, with low human development indicators. Many of their people still largely rely on rain-fed subsistence farming, leaving them particularly vulnerable to drought and erratic rainfall patterns. With the exception of Djibouti, which has almost no arable land, over three-quarters of these countries' populations earn their living through agriculture. Parts of the region are chronically food insecure. Aid groups suggest that while poor weather conditions have contributed to the scope of the current disaster, the humanitarian crisis also results from poor planning and policies that have made populations more vulnerable to drought.[16] In addition to providing emergency relief, the international community has responded to previous droughts in the region by establishing early warning systems and "safety nets" to mitigate the types of impact the poor climate conditions are having on the region. Without these mechanisms in place, experts say the current crisis would have been worse. However, rapidly rising food and fuel prices in the past year have left many families struggling to cope, and poor infrastructure and insecurity continue to limit humanitarian access in some areas.

Countries in the Horn

Somalia[17]

Terrorism, piracy, human trafficking, and the famine now affecting parts of southern Somalia are symptoms of the wider instability that has plagued Somalia since the collapse of the authoritarian Siad Barre regime in 1991. Somalia's internationally recognized Transitional Federal Government (TFG), established in 2004, remains unable to provide security or basic social services outside the capital, Mogadishu. The TFG is the most recent product of numerous domestic and international attempts to unite Somalia's regions, clans, and sub-clans within a credible central government (see Appendix D). The TFG has struggled in recent years to reconstitute national security and law enforcement entities and expand its authority outside Mogadishu, but factional fighting has continued.[18]

In 2007 a U.N.-mandated peacekeeping force, the African Union Mission in Somalia (AMISOM), began its peacekeeping operations in Somalia. It has been tasked with supporting political reconciliation, providing security for the TFG, and supporting the development of the Somali security forces. (For background information, see Appendix B.) As of September 2011, AMISOM had an estimated 9,000 troops in Somalia. Given competing security priorities and few resources, its role in facilitating humanitarian relief deliveries has been limited. The United States has played a primary role in supporting AMISOM since 2007.

Humanitarian, political, and security conditions continue to deteriorate across south-central Somalia. The TFG remains unable to provide security or basic social services outside the capital, Mogadishu. In early September 2011, the United Nations sponsored a consultative meeting in Mogadishu between the TFG and other Somali political stakeholders, who agreed on a roadmap toward a new constitution and elections in 2012.

Kenya[19]

Kenya, a nation of about 36.9 million people, has been an important ally of the United States for decades. While the country is relatively stable compared to its neighbors, a disputed election in December 2007 sparked violence that led to over 1,300 deaths, and communal conflict in parts of the country remains common. In April 2010, the Kenyan parliament passed a new draft constitution, and on August 4, 2010, Kenyans approved the new constitution. The next general elections are scheduled for 2012. Insufficient rains have led to poor crops and dying herds in parts of the country, and rising food and fuel prices have left many unable to meet basic needs. Kenya's central highlands are among Africa's most successful agricultural areas, but pastoral communities in vast arid areas of the north now face humanitarian conditions similar to those in Somalia. Kenya, like neighboring Uganda and Tanzania, relies on hydroelectric power for almost half of its electricity, and the drought has lowered water levels and resulted in power rationing throughout East Africa.

Ethiopia

One of Africa's largest countries with over 90 million people, Ethiopia has been plagued by internal unrest and frequent drought. The United States has been an important player in promoting democracy and dialogue between the government and opposition groups. The United States considers Ethiopia to be an important ally in a region marred by violence and instability. Concerns about human rights conditions and democracy nonetheless remain key issues in U.S.-Ethiopia relations. Despite a high rate of economic growth in recent years, its per capita income is among the world's lowest. The government continues to face ethnic insurgencies in parts of the country, including the Ogaden region near the border with Somalia, which is populated largely by ethnic Somalis. On May 23, 2010, millions of Ethiopians went to the polls to vote in national, regional, and local elections. The ruling party won all of the seats in the House of Representatives, except for two seats won by opposition members. The United States and the European Union declared that the elections were generally peaceful but did not meet international standards.

Eritrea

After a 30-year armed struggle against Ethiopia, Eritrea, gained independence in 1991. It is among the most authoritarian countries in the world. Political repression and human rights abuses have led many to emigrate. For most of the 1990s, the government of President Isaias Afewerki was considered a strong strategic U.S. ally in the Horn of Africa. Since the late 1990s, however, U.S. officials have expressed concern about a wide range of issues, including human rights conditions, Eritrea's role in Somalia, border disputes with Djibouti and Ethiopia, freedom of the press, and one-party rule. The country faces a U.N. arms embargo for its reported efforts to destabilize parts of the region, including Somalia, through reported support to Islamist insurgents. Eritrean officials have disputed reports of a humanitarian crisis in the country, stating that "There [are] no food shortages at the present time. Last year, we had a bumper harvest. We have also built up our reserves in terms of food stocks by importing food, so we will be ready for any emergency."[20]

Djibouti

Djibouti gained independence from France in June 1977. Hassan Gouled Aptidon, Djibouti's first head of state (1977-1999), contained ethnic tensions, provided a moderate standard of living to Djiboutians, and maintained a relatively open political system in an era when tyranny and Marxist military dictatorships dominated most of Africa. On April 8, 2011, Djibouti held presidential elections. The main opposition parties boycotted the election, claiming that it would be rigged. President Ismail Omar Guelleh won 80.63% of the votes, while his opponent won 19.37% of the votes cast.[21] The U.S. Combined Joint Task Force-Horn of Africa (CJTFHoA) is based in Djibouti at Camp Lemonier. In October 2008, Africa Command (AFRICOM) assumed command responsibility from CENTCOM. An estimated 2,000 U.S. military and civilian personnel make up CJTF-HoA. Djibouti also serves as one of the two locations worldwide for the USAID Food for Peace Program's storage facility.

INTERNATIONAL AND U.S. HUMANITARIAN RESPONSE

The United Nations, along with other partners, including the United States, has a strong presence in the Horn of Africa, and remains at the forefront of the current humanitarian response. All major U.N. relief agencies and international NGOs, together with dozens of smaller actors, are operating relief projects in the Horn. In Somalia, for example, between national and international staff, the humanitarian community has almost 900 people on the ground. International recovery efforts are typically complex because they require coordination among numerous different actors and international entities. In the current crisis, apart from U.N. agencies, those responding to the complex emergency include international organizations, non-governmental organizations (NGOs), private voluntary organizations (PVOs), and bilateral and multilateral donors.

Selected U.N. System Efforts

Humanitarian "clusters," or sectors focused on specific relief activities, are usually established during humanitarian crises to enable the United Nations to coordinate partners, prioritize resources, and facilitate planning. In the Horn of Africa region, clusters are led by various aid agencies or specific government ministries, and most have been in place for some time in response to the slow onset of the drought crisis. In Somalia and Ethiopia, all clusters are active. For example, in Somalia, U.N.-led clusters focus on a range of typical humanitarian activities including food aid, nutrition, health, shelter, water and sanitation, agriculture/livelihood, and protection. In Ethiopia, similar activities are led by the government and also include camp management, while humanitarian aid agencies focus on early warning, early recovery, and emergency telecommunications. There are no clusters in Djibouti; instead a humanitarian focal point has been assigned by the U.N. Development Program.[22] In Kenya, the clusters are the responsibility of the Kenyan government.

Although the Regional Head of Office for UNOCHA is based in Cairo, Egypt, the Horn of Africa humanitarian operation has been scaled up with the largest presence in Nairobi, Kenya, in part to gain access to Somalia. U.N. agencies have staff (international and national) in all affected countries, and humanitarian coordinators lead U.N. Country Teams in Somalia, Ethiopia, and Kenya.

The World Food Program (WFP) has estimated that as of September 15, 2011, more than 13 million people in the Horn are in need of food and other humanitarian assistance.[23] WFP has identified 9.6 million of the drought-affected population for near-term food assistance. Currently, WFP estimates that it is feeding about 7.4 million drought-affected people in the five Horn countries. (The shortfall is made up of people WFP cannot yet access in southern Somalia and drought-affected people in Kenya that it plans to reach in coming weeks.) Despite donor support for its humanitarian relief effort in the Horn, WFP says that $250 million of a total operation estimated to cost $760 million over the next six months remains unfunded.[24]

The Food and Agriculture Organization (FAO) of the United Nations organized an emergency meeting on July 25, 2011, in Rome, which included senior representatives from some of FAO's 191 member countries, other U.N. agencies, and international and non-governmental organizations. The meeting focused on the need for a "twin-track" program to avert the humanitarian crisis at hand and build long-term food security in the region. Governments of the six countries affected by the crisis agreed to continue to manage their response informed by the U.N. Inter-Agency Standing Committee's (IASC's) Horn of Africa Plan of Action. FAO currently operates relief and early recovery programs in all affected countries. Project proposals for drought relief activities are included in U.N. funding appeals for these countries.

Other donor coordination initiatives include an emergency summit held August 17, 2011, in Istanbul, Turkey, by the Organization of Islamic Cooperation (OIC), which pledged $350 million in aid to Somalia; and a donor conference sponsored by the African Union held on August 25 in Addis Ababa, Ethiopia, that raised $350 million, $300 million of which was from the Africa Development Bank. A donor conference to be hosted by the Gulf States is still to be confirmed. On the margins of the general debate of the 66th session of the U.N. General Assembly, UNOCHA organized a Ministerial Mini-Summit on the Humanitarian Response in the Horn of Africa on September 24, 2011, "to raise awareness of the scale and urgency of the humanitarian situation." The Mini-Summit resulted in new pledges of humanitarian aid totaling more than $218 million.[25]

Challenges of Access and Aid Delivery to Somalia

Many countries, including the United States, consider Somalia too dangerous to maintain a diplomatic presence in Mogadishu. Somalia presents humanitarian organizations with a complex set of challenges to aid delivery both in terms of poor infrastructure and insecurity. The country's infrastructure has been badly damaged by years of conflict. Roads are poorly maintained, and Somalia has few ports that can handle large cargo vessels.[26]

South-central Somalia is considered one of the most hostile environments in the world for aid workers, who are operating in an active conflict zone. Al Shabaab has obstructed the delivery of humanitarian assistance and directly threatened aid agencies. It also targets members of the TFG and AMISOM through guerrilla-style attacks and suicide bombings.[27] Absent a functioning central authority to enforce the rule of law, aid convoys traveling by road face numerous militia checkpoints and are subject to ad hoc "taxation," extortion, diversion of aid, and banditry, all of which have become increasingly frequent impediments to aid delivery since 2008.[28] Aircraft using the country's airports and landing strips have on occasion been vulnerable to attack.[29] Landmines and improvised explosive devices (IEDs) add to the dangers facing aid workers.

The security situation drove many international groups out of Al Shabaab-controlled areas by late 2009 and 2010. WFP, which Al Shabaab had accused of undermining Somali farmers by importing food, suspended operations in the south in January 2010 amid growing threats and intimidation, and Al Shabaab issued an official statement banning WFP from areas under its control the following month.[30] On July 5, 2011, Al Shabaab publicly requested international assistance for previously inaccessible southern Somalia.[31] The group's spokesperson later appeared to reverse the decision, announcing that aid agencies that were previously banned had "hidden agendas" and were not welcome, and accusing the United Nations of exaggerating the severity of the drought and politicizing the crisis.[32]

Since July, WFP has scaled up assistance and has begun to open new routes by land and air to serve famine-stricken areas. It began food aid airlifts to Mogadishu on July 27, 2011,[33] and reports that it has opened up a new logistics corridor to transport food supplies from Somaliland into Ethiopia and down to the Ethiopian border town of Dollo Ado. From there, food supplies can be transported across the border to people in southern Somalia.[34] In addition to logistical problems encountered in delivering food aid to food insecure, conflicted areas in Somalia, aid workers from WFP and other relief agencies are exposed to risks to their personal safety as well as risks to the food supplies being moved into the country. WFP reports that 14 of its aid workers have been killed in Somalia since 2008.

Other organizations have continued to operate in the south, including the Somali Red Crescent Society and the International Committee of the Red Cross (ICRC), and multiple Islamic aid organizations, which have reportedly faced strict conditions from local Al Shabaab officials, including a ban on female aid workers. Some international aid officials suggest that they have been able to continue operations through local partners, "if those delivering the aid are accepted by the local communities and if the aid is not linked to political or military agendas."[35] The TFG policy reportedly accepts whatever means are necessary to deliver food, including permitting local Muslim NGOs in Shabaab areas. The United States and other donors are also supporting cash-for-work and voucher programs in areas where humanitarian access is limited.

Somalia's TFG has accused Al Shabaab of deliberately starving people and preventing residents from leaving to seek assistance, and has called for international intervention. Other reports have reiterated concerns about Al Shabaab restrictions on aid in some areas.[36] The ability of some international aid groups to deliver aid in spite of contradictory statements by Al Shabaab officials might indicate what many analysts have long suspected: that Al Shabaab may not act as a monolithic entity and that some local commanders may continue to restrict aid while others may facilitate its delivery. Some reports suggest that differing views of Al Shabaab leaders on how to respond to the region's growing humanitarian needs may have led to, or widened, divisions within the group.[37]

Funding

U.N. Appeals

The bulk of donor funding comes through financial contributions or relief supplies to U.N. appeals. At the end of 2010, the United Nations issued several appeals for emergency financial assistance through its country teams in Kenya, Djibouti, and Somalia. Other funding mechanisms were created for Ethiopia and the Horn of Africa in general and are included in the chart in Appendix C. These appeals have been revised and updated and total more than $2.48 billion to support emergency food aid, health, water, sanitation, shelter, and other key needs, including early recovery efforts. As of September 20, 2011, commitments and contributions to the appeals of $1.55 billion have been received (which amounts to approximately 63% of all the appeals). In addition, the U.N. Central Emergency Response Fund (CERF) released $117.4 million to meet immediate humanitarian needs in Dijbouti, Ethiopia, Kenya, and Somalia.[38]

U.N. Secretary-General Ban Ki-moon and others have called on donor countries to contribute the additional funding currently required to meet expected needs.

Other Pledges and Contributions

Additional pledges and contributions have also been made outside these U.N. appeals through bilateral assistance to governments, international organizations, and NGOs. Some countries, including the U.S. government, are also providing assistance in the form of direct bilateral assistance. Funding has also been provided to organizations operating outside of the U.N. appeal. As of September 20, 2011, uncommitted pledges that may be available for the appeals total $976.4 million.[39]

While funding provided for the humanitarian crisis is made up of both appeal and non-appeal contributions, an up-to-date record of all international contributions is not available—in part because some assistance is not reported to governments or coordinating agencies, and in part because of the delay in their recording.

Although aid agencies fault Al Shabaab for the non-permissive environment in southern Somalia, some observers have also criticized Western donors for not providing adequate resources for the humanitarian response in Somalia. Many experts would agree the funding situation in the near term has improved, but concerns remain about sustaining support through the crisis, which is expected to last well into 2012.[40] The U.N. Monitoring Group on Somalia and Eritrea, whose mandate includes reporting on the obstruction of humanitarian assistance to Somalia, stated in a June 2011 report that, in addition to threats from elements of Al Shabaab, which it characterized as the "single greatest obstacle to humanitarian access in Somalia,"

> Exogenous factors contributing to this harsh environment included a substantial overall decrease in international funding, and donor Government regulations restricting operations and access.... Besides restrictions imposed by Al-Shabaab, most organizations and agencies said that the greatest impediment to humanitarian assistance in Somalia was and continued to be inadequate funding.[41]

The Monitoring Group noted that there was a "substantial overall decrease" in international funding for humanitarian assistance to Somalia in 2010.

While total amounts contributed by private citizens are not available, they are thought to be low compared to other crises, and initiatives to raise awareness about the crisis and fundraising campaigns are ongoing.[42] In an effort to create broader engagement by the American public USAID launched the Famine, War, Drought (FWD) relief campaign in coordination with the Ad Council. The U.S. government is working with NGOs, the United Nations, and diaspora communities to bring attention to the enormity and severity of the crisis while seeking to increase private donations.[43]

U.S. Humanitarian Efforts

The U.S. State Department has said that it is focusing not only on a response to address short-term needs and save lives, but also to build capacity to reduce the cycles of famine and failure that occur repeatedly in the Horn region. In the past year, in coordination with the international community, the U.S. government has worked to preposition food stocks in the region, increase funding for early warning systems, and strengthen assistance in other sectors, such as health, water, and sanitation. The U.S. government reissued or renewed a number of U.S. disaster declarations in countries in the Horn in response to the ongoing complex emergencies. On July 6, 2011, through its Office of Foreign Disaster Assistance (OFDA), USAID activated a regional Disaster Assistance Response Team (DART) in Nairobi, Kenya, and Addis Ababa, Ethiopia. It also set up an interagency task force to coordinate and facilitate the humanitarian response to the drought crisis through the Washington, DC-based Response Management Team (RMT).

The United States is the largest bilateral donor of emergency assistance to the eastern Horn of Africa. As of September 15, 2011, USAID reported that the United States had provided $604.6 million of humanitarian assistance thus far in FY2011, of which $403.3 million (68%) was emergency food aid.[44] Those funds have financed the provision of 414,000 metric tons of food distributed by WFP throughout the region and by Catholic Relief Services (CRS) in Ethiopia. U.S. food aid has been made available primarily through Food for Peace Title II (Emergency Assistance) or from International Disaster Assistance (IDA)-funded Emergency Food Assistance for Drought-Affected Areas.

In the longer term, the United States is focusing its aid on helping countries in the Horn build safety net programs and develop their agricultural sectors. For example, Ethiopia's Productive Safety Net Program (PSNP) provides food and cash to an estimated 7.5 million Ethiopians in exchange for work building community assets such as roads, schools, and clinics. The main U.S. input into this multi-donor financed project is commodity food aid provided as Food for Peace Act Title II nonemergency food aid.[45] USAID's Feed the Future (FtF) program, initiated in 2009 as a major foreign aid initiative, is developing approaches to agriculture in the Horn that address hunger and food insecurity.[46] In Kenya, for example, the United States is assisting in a multi-year agricultural development program under FtF that aims to support Kenyan investment in staple food value chain development, including livestock and livestock products; rural finance; policy analysis, advocacy, and capacity-building; agricultural research and technology transfer; and water and sanitation.[47]

Restrictions on Aid

A number of experts and policymakers are concerned that, on the one hand, existing donor restrictions, including U.S. sanctions, may be impacting the effective delivery of aid in Somalia and the recipients for whom the aid is intended. On the other hand, donors are also worried that aid delivered to the region may benefit Al Shabaab, which is classified by the U.S. government as a Foreign Terrorist Organization (FTO), included in the United States' Specially Designated Global Terrorist (SDGT) list under authorities enacted in the aftermath of the 2001 terrorist attacks, and identified by both the United States and the United Nations as an entity contributing to the conflict in Somalia (Executive Order 13536 and U.N. Security Council resolution 1844 (2008)). Al Shabaab reportedly earns significant revenues from taxation in southern Somalia, and it has not considered aid agencies exempt from its revenue generating efforts. The group has reportedly demanded registration fees and extorted bribes from aid groups, stolen aid shipments, and, in some cases, benefited from the transport contracts of international aid organizations. Aid agencies have expressed concern that they may be exposed to prosecution in the United States if they deliver aid in Al Shabaab-controlled areas, as the capture or use of humanitarian aid by Al Shabaab could potentially violate the U.S. government's "strict liability" standard against providing material support to terrorists.[48] The U.N. Monitoring Group notes these concerns in its June 2011 report.

In 2009, questions were raised within the U.S. government as to whether, under its Somalia sanctions regulations, a license was required for the State Department and USAID to undertake humanitarian, development, and peacekeeping assistance programs authorized by the Secretary of State in Somalia. After receiving input on this question from the U.S. Treasury Department's Office of Foreign Assets Control (OFAC), USAID subsequently directed its contractors and grantees to perform "enhanced due diligence" to avoid violating existing U.S. sanctions. In response to the USAID directives, several USAID grantees operating in southern Somalia expressed concern that requirements to report violations, unintentional or otherwise, by staff and sub-grantees, to the U.S. government could open them to U.S. prosecution.

USAID funding for NGOs to deliver humanitarian aid in south-central Somalia stalled during this period. In addition, according to USAID, NGOs conducting activities with U.S. funding in northern Somalia were specifically precluded through their grant provisions from carrying out activities in Al Shabaab-controlled areas of southern Somalia. USAID implementing partners report that grant processing for new programs, even in northern and central Somalia, was suspended for nearly eight months of FY2011, in spite of warnings about the pending crisis.

Some Members of Congress have sought clarification of the sanctions-licensing issue as well as the Administration's policy decisions about the delivery of humanitarian assistance in Somalia as a whole.[49] In August 2011, the Obama Administration eased some of the restrictions impacting aid delivery.[50]

U.N. Sanctions[51]

Beginning in 2008, the U.N. Security Council has targeted individuals and entities who engage in or support "acts that threaten the peace, security or stability of Somalia;" violate the arms embargo;[52] or obstruct the delivery of, access to, or distribution of humanitarian assistance in Somalia (S/RES/1844 (2008), November 20, 2008). Member states are required to block entry into or transit through their jurisdictions of designees (paras. 1, 2), and freeze the funds, financial assets, and economic resources in their jurisdictions of designated individuals and entities (paras. 3, 4). Al Shabaab and several of its top leaders are among those designated. In March 2010, the Security Council authorized member states to make available for one year funds, assets, or other economic resources that would be subject to blocking under the 2008 resolution, "to ensure the timely delivery of urgently needed humanitarian assistance in Somalia, by the United Nations, its specialized agencies or programmes, humanitarian organizations having observer status with the United Nations General Assembly that provide humanitarian assistance, or their implementing partners" (S/RES/1916 (2010), March 19, 2010). The resolution also required the U.N. Humanitarian Aid Coordinator for Somalia to report quarterly on both the implementation of this humanitarian exemption and impediments to delivery of humanitarian assistance. A year later, the Security Council extended the exemption to meet the humanitarian crisis and related reporting, now to be filed by the Emergency Relief Coordinator, for another 16 months (S/RES/1972 (2011, March 17, 2011), through mid-July 2012. Most recently, to condemn the obstruction of humanitarian aid delivery and attacks on humanitarian workers by armed groups as the famine conditions worsen, the Security Council expanded the terms of the 2008 embargo to target individuals and entities whose actions threaten the peace, security, or stability of Somalia, violate the arms embargo, obstruct humanitarian aid delivery, recruit child soldiers, or target civilians for violence, abduction, or displacement (S/RES/2002 (2011), July 29, 2011). The latest resolution, however, also reinforces the authority of member states to provide humanitarian assistance through July 2012.

ISSUES FOR CONGRESS

Budget Priorities: Global Humanitarian Accounts

Humanitarian assistance generally receives strong bipartisan congressional support and the United States is typically a leader and major contributor to relief efforts in humanitarian disasters.[53] When disasters require immediate emergency relief, the Administration may fund pledges by depleting its disaster accounts intended for worldwide use throughout a fiscal year. That aid is drawn from existing funds. The international community is also making substantial donations toward meeting immediate needs.

Amid efforts to tackle rising budget deficits by, among other measures, slowing or reducing discretionary spending, finding the resources to sustain U.S. aid pledges may be difficult. For example, after the 2004 Indian Ocean tsunami disaster, some Members of Congress publicly expressed concern that funding for tsunami relief and reconstruction, which depleted most worldwide disaster contingency accounts, could jeopardize resources for subsequent international disasters or for other aid priorities from which tsunami emergency aid had been transferred. These accounts were fully restored through supplemental appropriations. At the time, others noted the substantial size of American private donations for tsunami victims and argued that because of other budget pressures, the United States government did not need to transfer additional aid beyond what was already pledged. In Haiti, disaster accounts were drawn down to provide relief following the earthquake in 2010. The relief funding in the FY2010 supplemental request reimbursed funding provided or obligated. If global humanitarian accounts are not replenished following a humanitarian crisis or disaster, U.S. capacity to respond to other emergencies could be impacted. Congress may reevaluate and revise priorities and approaches of U.S. assistance to the Horn of Africa.

Budget Priorities: Food Aid

U.S. international relief and development agencies and hunger advocacy groups have raised concerns about cuts in funds for international food aid in the FY2011 continuing resolution (CR, P.L. 112-10), and in the House-passed FY2012 agriculture appropriations bill (H.R. 2112).[54] While not disputing the case for long-term deficit reduction, these groups argue that "protecting spending on the most vulnerable is the right thing to do." The FY2011 CR reduced international food aid by over 18% (measuring the FY2011 appropriations against the FY2010 enacted food aid total). H.R. 2112, if enacted, would further reduce U.S. food aid funding in FY2012. The House FY2012 agriculture appropriations bill cuts food aid by about a third, from its FY2011 enacted amount ($1.5 billion) to $1.049 billion. The Senate has scheduled markup on its version of FY2012 agriculture appropriations. The House also has taken steps toward reducing funding for the Development Assistance (DA) account, the major source of funds for USAID's long-term agricultural development and food security assistance (such as the Feed the Future Initiative). The House Appropriations Foreign Operations Subcommittee draft bill for FY2012 foreign affairs spending proposes to reduce funds for DA by 18% below the FY2011 level.[55]

Diversion of Food Aid

In March 2010, the U.N. Sanctions Monitoring Group on Somalia suggested that internal WFP contracting procedures "create an environment conducive to large-scale diversion of food aid and warrant further, independent investigation."[56] The Monitoring Group subsequently reported in July 2011 that WFP has since taken steps to improve accountability and transparency in its food distribution, especially in Mogadishu. Responding to more recent press reports that food aid was being diverted from essential feeding operations and being sold in local markets in Mogadishu, WFP announced that it is investigating instances of diversion and that it has been taking steps to ensure "that food assistance is carefully tracked and accountability is strengthened."[57] The scale of diversion has not been ascertained, although there have been reported allegations that "a massive amount of food aid is being stolen."[58] One U.S. organization has called for congressional hearings to look into the issue of aid theft and efforts to prevent it.[59]

Restrictions on U.S. Aid

On July 29, 2011, the Obama Administration issued new guidance to provide greater flexibility in U.S. sanctions to ensure that aid workers implementing U.S.-funded programs in Al Shabaabcontrolled areas of Somalia are not in conflict with U.S. laws and regulations. To date, the new guidance applies only to State and USAID-funded programs. The NGO community has welcomed efforts to ease the legal restrictions on U.S-funded programs, but has expressed concern that aid groups might still be open to penalties under U.S. sanctions if they were inadvertently to provide some benefit to Al Shabaab while delivering aid from other funding sources (e.g., the European Union or private charitable contributions), even if that funding was provided through the U.N. Consolidated Appeals Process.[60] Administration officials have stressed that NGOs subject to U.S. jurisdiction that are not operating under U.S. government grants or contracts must ensure that their programs are consistent with U.S. legal requirements restricting transactions with Al Shabaab in the course of providing aid in Somalia. The U.S. NGO community has argued that some transactions, such as the payment of registration or checkpoint fees or taxes on local staff or partners, may be unavoidable and that the current legal and licensing framework does not give sufficient authorization or assurances to groups seeking to deliver aid in Al Shabaab-controlled areas.[61]

Burdensharing and Donor Fatigue

The drought in the Horn of Africa has received worldwide attention from governments, particularly in the last few months, but the focus by the general public appears to have been intermittent. The governments in the region, the United States, the United Nations, and many others have asked for and encouraged donor contributions. It is not always evident whether figures listing donor amounts represent pledges of support or more specific obligations.[62] Pledges made by governments do not necessarily result in actual contributions. It also cannot be assumed that the funds committed to relief actually represent new contributions, since the money may previously have been allocated elsewhere. It will take time for a more complete picture to reveal how the actual costs of the unfolding crisis in the Horn will be shared among international donors. Comparing USG and international aid is also difficult because of the often dramatically different forms the assistance takes (in-kind contributions vs. cash, for instance). Moreover, as the situation stabilizes, and early recovery efforts get underway in 2012, sustaining donor interest (and commitment to honor existing pledges) could be a challenge. This task is only compounded by the need to maintain funding priorities and secure funds needed for other disaster areas worldwide amid an uncertain global economy.

LOOKING AHEAD

The drought currently plaguing the Horn of Africa region has triggered what is considered one of the worst international humanitarian crises in 60 years. At the close of the U.N. Mini-Summit in late September 2011, organizers lauded that $2.48 billion had been pledged but asserted that another $500 million would be required to address critical needs in the near term. The United States is the largest single bilateral donor to meet this emergency at a time when it faces its own substantial budgetary pressures.

No one can predict the weather, so no one can state with any certainty when the drought-driven factors of the crisis will end. The humanitarian crisis is not caused solely by natural disaster, however. Internal conflicts and conflicts between and among states are major contributing factors. Delivering humanitarian food, medicine, and fuel is never easy or unfettered. The Horn of Africa region, however, offers up its own unique set of challenges. Areas of Somalia, in particular, stand out for their complicating factors. How to effectively and efficiently deliver life-saving assistance in an environment of pirates, bandits, terrorists, poor-to-nonexistent infrastructure, and a poor-to-nonfunctioning state, is the riddle the United States and its international partners strive to solve.

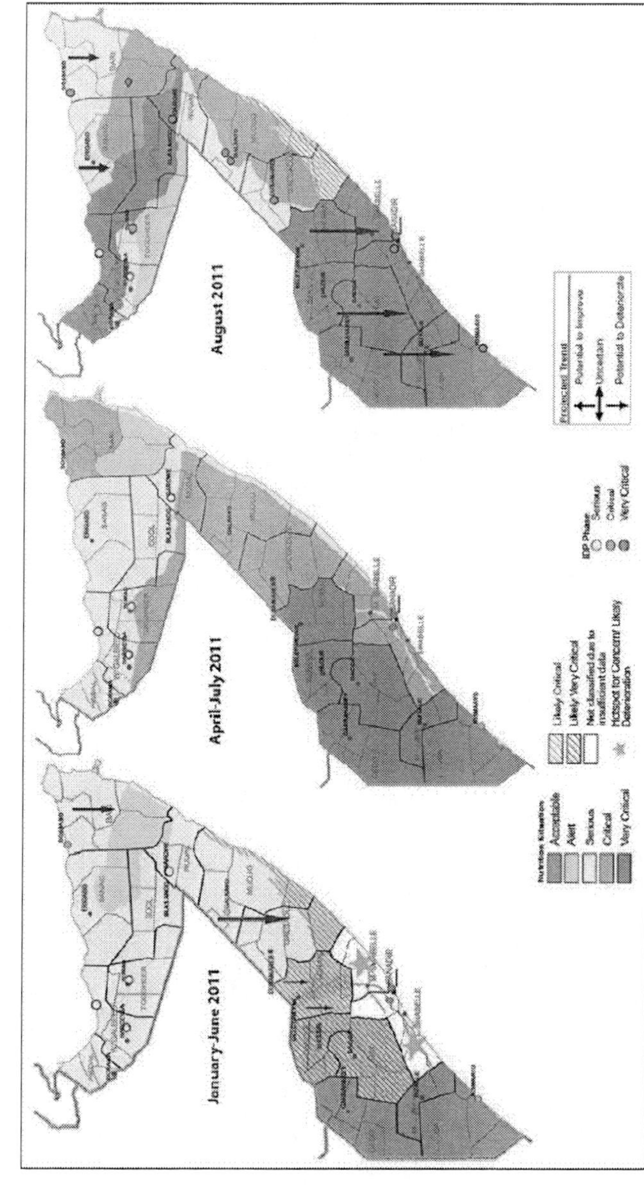

Source: Food Security and Nutrition Analysis Unit (FSNAU), adapted by CRS.

Figure A-1. Map of Somalia.

APPENDIX B. AFRICAN UNION MISSION IN SOMALIA (AMISOM)

The AU Mission in Somalia's (AMISOM's) current mandate is outlined in U.N. Security Council Resolution 1772 (2007) as follows:

1) to support dialogue and reconciliation in Somalia by assisting with the free movement, safe passage, and protection of those involved in the political dialogue;
2) to provide protection to the Transitional Federal Institutions to help them carry out government functions and to provide security for key infrastructure;
3) to assist within its capabilities in the re-establishment and training of all-inclusive Somali security forces;
4) to contribute, as requested and within its capabilities, to the creation of the necessary security conditions for the provision of humanitarian aid; and
5) to protect its personnel, facilities, installations, equipment and mission, and to ensure the security and freedom of movement of its personnel.

The U.N. Security Council, under Resolution 1964 (2010), authorized the mission to increase its troop size from 8,000 to 12,000 and extended AMISOM's mandate through September 30, 2011. On September 30, 2011, the Security Council unanimously adopted Resolution 2010 (2011) extending its authorization of AMISOM until October 31, 2012.[63] The resolution supported achievement of the authorized level of 12,000 troops and encouraged development of a guard force within AMISOM's mandated troop levels to provide security, escort, and protection services to personnel from the international community. It also expressed the Council's intention to review the possible need to adjust troop levels of AMISOM once the mission reaches its mandated level.

The African Union has sought to further increase the mission's troop levels and has requested that the U.N. Security Council impose a no-fly zone and naval blockade on Somalia. Finding countries willing to commit troops, however, has been a challenge. With renewal of the AMISOM mandate, Sierra Leone, Djibouti, and South Sudan have pledged to deploy troops to AMISOM in 2012.

APPENDIX C. FUNDING STATUS OF U.N. APPEALS FOR HORN OF AFRICA CRISIS (AS OF SEPTEMBER 20, 2011)

Table C-1. Funding Status for Horn of Africa Crisis
(All figures in U.S.$)

Appeal	Updated Revised Requirements	Funding to Date	Percent Funded	Unmet Requirements	Uncommitted Pledges (that may be applied to the Appeals)
Kenya Appeal	$741 million	$476.7 million	64%	$264.3 million	$69.1 million
Djibouti Drought Appeal	$33,3 million	$18.7 million	56%	$14.6 million	$0 million
Somalia Consolidated Appeal Process	$1.1 billion	$677.8 million	64%	$384.9 million	$633.8 million
Ethiopia Humanitarian Requirements (July-December 2011) plus refugee requirements	$644.4 million	$304.8 million	46%	$339.6 million	$29.6 million
Pledges for general funding for agencies in appeals, country not specified	n/a	$76.6 million	n/a	n/a	n/a
Pledges and funding for crisis not yet country or appeal-specific					$243.9 million
Total	$2.48 billion	$1.55 billion	63%	$927 million	$976.4 million
Ethiopia funding received against Jan-Jun 2011 requirements	n/a	$182 million	n/a	n/a	n/a
Grand Total of Appeal Contributions	n/a	$1.74 billion	n/a	n/a	n/a

Source: U.N. Office for the Coordination of Humanitarian Affairs, *Horn of Africa Drought Crisis Fact Sheet*, September 20, 2011.

Note: There is no formal U.N. appeal for Ethiopia. Funding combines humanitarian and refugee related requirements. Funding to date divided into two 6 month periods in 2011 by arrangement with Government of Ethiopia.

APPENDIX D.
HISTORICAL BACKGROUND AND
U.S. POLICY IN THE HORN OF AFRICA

Overview and Contributing Factors to the Crises

The Horn of Africa is by far the most unstable region in Sub-Saharan Africa. This region has been marred by civil wars, internal political turmoil, inter-state wars, famine, and man-made humanitarian disasters in recent decades. The Horn has also emerged as a region that is highly vulnerable to terrorist attacks and is considered a safe haven for international terrorist groups. The humanitarian crises in the Horn of Africa are not caused solely by natural disasters. Internal conflicts and conflicts between states are major contributing factors to humanitarian crises. Moreover, a range of other factors, such as high rates of poverty, unemployment, and population growth; scarce resources and economic mismanagement; and interference in the internal affairs of neighboring countries, corruption, and poor leadership also play significant roles in deteriorating conditions.

Efforts to resolve the number of conflicts in the Horn have led to important peace agreements, but these agreements have not contributed to lasting peace and stability. For example, Ethiopia and Somalia have fought major wars in recent decades. Eritrea and Ethiopia were at war in 1998- 2000, in which over 100,000 people were killed and many more displaced. They remain at war, despite a peace agreement signed in 2000. Somalia is in a state of anarchy, despite a peace agreement reached in 2004 that led to the formation of the Transitional Federal Government (TFG). The Council of Islamic Courts (CIC) took control of Mogadishu in June 2006. Ethiopia's intervention in December 2006 to oust the CIC and install the TFG in Mogadishu made Somalia more unstable than it was during the six months the CIC was in power.

Conflict and Famine in Somalia in the Early 1990s

In Somalia, United Nations officials and human rights groups have long considered humanitarian conditions among the worst in the world. It has been marred by factional fighting and humanitarian disasters since the collapse of the central government in 1991, when famine and lawlessness ensued, and an estimated 300,000 Somalis died of starvation during the civil war that followed. After lengthy delays, due to security concerns in 1992, the U.N.

Security Council established the United Nations Operation in Somalia (UNOSOM I) to facilitate humanitarian relief. The deteriorating security situation eventually left the U.N. mission unable to deliver food and supplies to those in need and led to a U.N. appeal for military support for the humanitarian operation.

The role of the United Nations and United States in Somalia entered a new stage in December 1992, when the Council, acting under Chapter VII, authorized the Secretary-General and U.N. member states, under U.S. command to "use all necessary means to establish ... a secure environment for humanitarian relief operations in Somalia." The Council provided for liaison between this operation, named the Unified Task Force (UNITAF), and UNOSOM I.

In December 1992, President George H. W. Bush ordered 25,000 U.S. troops into Somalia as part of a major coalition operation under U.S.-led UNITAF, named Operation Restore Hope by the United States. Experts believe U.S. and international intervention at the time saved many lives and averted a major humanitarian disaster. When President Bill Clinton took office in January 1993, he reduced American involvement. In March 1993, the Council expanded the size and mandate for the U.N. Operation in Somalia, designating it UNOSOM II. The United States transferred command of UNITAF to UNOSOM II; U.S. troops remained in Somalia. The deaths of 18 American soldiers in a firefight with forces of General Mohammed Farah Aideed in October 1993, along with congressional pressure, prompted the Clinton Administration to end U.S. participation in peacekeeping in Somalia. U.S. troops left Somalia in March 1994, and the UNOSOM II ended its mission in the spring of 1995.

Somalia in the Decades after the 1990s Famine

In October 2002, the Inter-Governmental Authority for Development (IGAD), led by the government of Kenya, launched a peace process designed to end factional fighting in Somalia. In September 2003, the parties agreed on a Transitional National Charter (TNC). In August 2004, a 275-member Somali Transitional Parliament was inaugurated in Kenya. In October 2004, Parliament elected Abdullahi Yusuf Ahmed as the new president of Somalia. In June 2006, the forces of the Islamic Courts Union (ICU) took control of the capital, Mogadishu. During the six-month rule by the ICU, Mogadishu became relatively peaceful, but efforts to bring peace did not lead to a major breakthrough. On December 28, 2006, Ethiopian troops captured Mogadishu with little resistance from the ICU. In 2008, fighting between insurgent groups and Ethiopian-Somali Transitional Federal Government (TFG) forces intensified, and by late 2008, the TFG had lost control of most of south-central Somalia to insurgent groups. In late December 2008, President Yusuf resigned from office and left for Yemen. In January 2009, the Somali Parliament elected the leader of the Alliance for the Re-Liberation of Somalia (ARS), Sheikh Sharif Sheikh Ahmad, as president. In January 2009, Ethiopian forces completed their withdrawal from Somalia.

U.S. Policy in Previous Crises in the Horn of Africa

The United States has been actively engaged in the Horn of Africa region for over 50 years. The United States and Ethiopia established diplomatic relations in 1903 and have maintained good relations, except during the military dictatorship under Mengistu Haile Mariam in the 1970s and 1980s. The United States also had relations with the Siad Barre government in Somalia, although relations were poor for most of the 1980s. In recent decades, the United States has played key roles in conflict resolution and provided significant humanitarian assistance. The United States was actively engaged in 1991 in Ethiopia after the collapse of the Mengistu regime and later in mediating the border dispute between Eritrea and Ethiopia. U.S. engagement in Somalia, however, has been marginal and largely influenced by counter-terrorism concerns over the past decade, although the Obama Administration has been actively engaged in support of the TFG. Relations between Eritrea and the United States are currently poor. Relations between Ethiopia and the United States are strong, although some Members of Congress have been critical of Ethiopia's human rights record and the government's handling of the 2005 and 2010 elections.

Some Members of Congress have also actively followed issues in the Horn of Africa and traveled frequently to the region. At the height of the humanitarian crisis in Somalia in 1992, Congress held nine hearings and later passed the Horn of Africa Recovery and Food Security Act, which was the most far-reaching legislation on Africa in the 102nd Congress. In 1992, then-Senator Nancy Kassebaum argued for more active U.S. engagement in Somalia and called for the United Nations to appoint a Special Envoy. Kassebaum and Senator Paul Simon traveled to Somalia in July 1992 and upon their return recommended that the United Nations send a peacekeeping force to Somalia, with or without the consent of the warlords. The Select Committee on Hunger and the Senate and House subcommittees on Africa were very active on political, humanitarian, and human rights issues in the Horn of Africa region. Congress remains active in following events in the Horn of Africa. The House and Senate subcommittees on Africa held several hearings in the 111th Congress and passed a number of legislative proposals focused on Horn countries; the 112th Congress has held several hearings.

APPENDIX E.
THE U.S. GOVERNMENT EMERGENCY RESPONSE MECHANISM FOR INTERNATIONAL DISASTERS

The United States is generally a leader and major contributor to relief efforts in response to humanitarian disasters. The President has broad authority to provide emergency assistance for foreign disasters and the U.S. government provides disaster assistance through several U.S. agencies. The very nature of humanitarian disasters—the need to respond quickly in order to save lives and provide relief—has resulted in a rather unrestricted definition of what this type of assistance consists of at both a policy and an operational level. While humanitarian assistance is assumed to provide for urgent food, shelter, and medical needs, the agencies within the U.S. government providing this support typically expand or contract the definition in response to circumstances. Funds may be used for U.S. agencies to deliver services or to provide grants to international organizations (IOs), international governmental and non-governmental organizations (NGOs), and private or religious voluntary organizations (PVOs). The U.S. Agency for International Development (USAID) is the U.S. government agency charged with coordinating U.S. government and private sector assistance. It also coordinates with international organizations, the governments of countries suffering disasters, and other governments.

The Office of Foreign Disaster Assistance (OFDA) in USAID's Bureau for Democracy, Conflict and Humanitarian Assistance (DCHA) provides immediate relief materials and personnel, many of whom are already abroad on mission. It is responsible for providing non-food humanitarian assistance and can quickly assemble Disaster Assistance Response Teams (DARTs) to assess conditions. OFDA has wide authority to borrow funds, equipment, and personnel from other parts of USAID and other federal agencies. USAID has two other offices that administer U.S. humanitarian aid: Food For Peace (FFP) and the Office of Transition Initiatives (OTI). USAID administers emergency food aid under FFP (Title II of P.L. 480) and provides relief and development food aid that does not have to be repaid. OTI provides post-disaster transition assistance, which includes mainly short-term peace and democratization projects with some attention to humanitarian elements but not emergency relief.

Although not currently applicable to the Horn of Africa crisis, the Department of Defense (DOD) Overseas Humanitarian, Disaster and Civic Aid (OHDACA) funds three Dodd humanitarian programs: the Humanitarian Assistance Program (HAP), Humanitarian Mine Action (HMA) Program, and Foreign Disaster Relief and Emergency Response (FDR/ER). OHDACA provides humanitarian support to stabilize emergency situations and deals with a range of tasks including providing food, shelter and supplies, and medical evacuations. In addition the President has the authority to draw down defense equipment and direct military personnel to respond to disasters. The President may also use the Denton program to provide space-available transportation on military aircraft and ships to private donors who wish to transport humanitarian goods and equipment in response to a disaster.

Generally, OFDA provides emergency assistance for 30 to 90 days after a disaster. The same is true for Department of Defense humanitarian assistance. After the initial emergency is over, assistance is provided through other channels, such as the regular country development programs of USAID.

The State Department also administers programs for humanitarian relief with a focus on refugees and the displaced. The Emergency Refugee and Migration Account (ERMA) is a contingency fund that provides wide latitude to the President in responding to refugee emergencies. Assistance to address emergencies lasting more than a year comes out of the regular Migration and Refugee Account (MRA) through the Population, Migration and Refugees (PRM) bureau. PRM assists refugees worldwide, conflict victims, and populations of concern to the United Nations High Commissioner for Refugees (UNHCR), often extended to include internally displaced people (IDPs). Humanitarian assistance includes a range of services from basic needs to community services.

APPENDIX F. CONGRESSIONAL ACTION

Legislation in the 112th Congress Focused on the Horn of Africa Crisis

H.Res. 361

This resolution commends the contributions of the U.S. government in responding to the drought and famine in the Horn of Africa region, as well as creating a 5-year program in areas of Somalia to promote stability, mitigate conflict and strengthen relations between residents and their government. The resolution also calls on the U.S. government to continue to provide resources to the region to alleviate poverty and hunger and to provide long-term development assistance. This resolution was introduced on July 20, 2011, and referred to the House Committee on Foreign Affairs.

H.R. 2112

The Agriculture, Rural Development, Food and Drug Administration, and Related Agencies Appropriations Act, 2012 includes $1,040,198,000 for Food for Peace Title II grants as passed by the House on June 16, 2011. S.Rept. 112-73, issued on September 7, 2011, by the Senate Committee on Appropriations, recommends an appropriation of $1,562,000,000 for the grants, and cites the famine in the Horn of Africa region, as well as an increase in the price of food and transportation, to justify the increased amount.

Congressional Hearings Focused on the Horn of Africa Crisis

"Outlook in Somalia," House Committee on Foreign Affairs, Subcommittee on Africa, Global Health and Human Rights and Subcommittee on Terrorism, Nonproliferation, and Trade, July 7, 2011.

"U.S.-Africa Defense and Security Partnership," House Committee on Foreign Affairs, Subcommittee on Africa, Global Health and Human Rights, July 26, 2011.

"Drought and Famine in the Horn of Africa," Senate Committee on Foreign Relations, Subcommittee on African Affairs, August 3, 2011.

"USAID's Long-Term Strategy for Addressing East African Emergencies," House Committee on Foreign Affairs, Subcommittee on Africa, Global Health, and Human Rights, September 8, 2011.

APPENDIX G. LINKS FOR FURTHER INFORMATION ABOUT THE HORN OF AFRICA HUMANITARIAN CRISIS

U.S. Government Agencies

United States Agency for International Development (USAID)
http://www.usaid.gov/hornofafrica
Provides a list of non-government organizations (NGOs) that accept donations for relief efforts. Also provides information on the U.S. response to the crisis with fact sheets and maps.
http://www.usaid.gov/fwd
Provides detailed facts and information about the crisis.
Embassy of the United States, Addis Ababa, Ethiopia
http://ethiopia.usembassy.gov/news-events/horn-of-africa-drought
Horn of Africa Drought: U.S. Response: a compilation of official statements, fact sheets, and maps prepared by the U.S. government.
Famine Early Warning Systems Network (FEWS NET)
http://www.fews.net/Pages/default.aspx
U.S. Mission to the United Nations and Other International Organizations in Geneva http://geneva.usmission.gov/category/humanitarian/

United Nations

Food and Agriculture Organization of the United Nations (FAO)
http://www.fao.org/crisis/horn-africa/home/en/
IRIN News
a service of the United Nations Office for the Coordination of Humanitarian Affairs: http://www.irinnews.org/
United Nations Children's Fund (UNICEF)
UNICEF in Eritrea: http://www.unicef.org/infobycountry/eritrea.html
UNICEF in Ethiopia: http://www.unicef.org/infobycountry/ethiopia.html
UNICEF in Kenya: http://www.unicef.org/infobycountry/kenya.html
UNICEF in Somalia: http://www.unicef.org/infobycountry/somalia.html
UNICEF USA Fund: http://www.unicefusa.org/work/emergencies/horn-of-africa/ United Nations High Commissioner for Refugees
http://www.unhcr.org/pages/4e1ff4b06.html

United Nations Office for the Coordination of Humanitarian Affairs (OCHA) http://www.unocha.org/crisis/horn-africa-crisis
World Food Programme
http://www.wfp.org/crisis/horn-of-africa

Red Cross Movement

The American Red Cross
http://www.redcross.org/portal/site/en/rco_search?q=africa
The International Committee of the Red Cross
http://www.icrc.org/eng/where-we-work/africa/somalia/index.jsp
The International Federation of Red Cross and Red Crescent Societies http://www.ifrc.org/news-and-media

Other Resources

Action Against Hunger http://www.actionagainsthunger.org/blog/updates-our-work-horn-africa-focus-somalia African Development Bank
http://www.afdb.org/en/
American Jewish World Service
http://ajws.org/
BBC News
East Africa Hunger Crisis http://www.bbc.co.uk/news/world-africa-14248278

CARE
http://www.care.org/campaigns
Catholic Relief Services
http://crs.org/emergency
CHF International http://www.chfinternational.org/node/36358
Christian Reformed World Relief Committee (CRWRC)
http://www.crcna.org/pages/crwrc_idr_eadrought.cfm
Episcopal Relief & Development
http://www.er-d.org/EastAfricaResponseAugust2011
Food Security and Nutrition Analysis Unit – Somalia (FSNAU)
http://www.fsnau.org/The Hunger Project
http://www.thp.org/where_we_work/africa/ethiopia/overivew

InterAction
http://www.interaction.org/horn-of-africa-crisis
International Medical Corps
http://internationalmedicalcorps.org/page.aspx?pid=376
Islamic Relief USA http://www.irusa.org/emergencies/east-africa-crisis/
Lutheran World Relief
http://lwr.org/site/c.dmJXKiOYJgI6G/b.7549057/k.7558/East_Africa
Medecins sans Frontieres (Doctors without Borders)
http://www.msf.org/ Mercy Corps
http://www.mercycorps.org/hornofafricahungercrisis
Oxfam International
http://www.oxfam.org/eastafrica
Relief International
https://www.ri.org/newsroom/news-article.php?ID
Relief Web
http://reliefweb.int/horn-africa-crisis2011
Provides updated fact sheets, news, and maps issued by a variety of
organizations. Save the Children
http://www.savethechildren.org/site/c.8rKLIXMGIpI4E/b.7539035/k.B9FB/
Africa_Drought_Sparks_Food_Shortage_Child_Hunger_and_Humanitarian_C
risis.htm
World Bank
http://www.worldbank.org/foodcrisis/
World Concern
http://www.worldconcern.org/crisis/
World Vision http://www.worldvision.org/#/home/main/hunger-drought

End Notes

[1] For the United Nations to officially declare a famine, three important conditions must be met. First, 20% of the population must have fewer than 2100 kilocalories of food available per day. Secondly, more than 30% of children must be acutely malnourished. And finally, 2 deaths per day in every 10,000 people—or 4 deaths per day in every 10,000 children—must be caused by lack of food.

[2] Famine Early Warning Systems Network and the Food Security and Nutrition Analysis Unit, "Famine Thresholds Surpassed in Three New Areas of Southern Somalia," August 3, 2011. These areas included Balcad and Cadale districts of Middle Shabelle, the Afgooye corridor IDP settlement, and the Mogadishu IDP settlement. On September 5, famine was declared in Bay region.

[3] For updated information on humanitarian needs and responses by country in the Horn, see UNOCHA "Horn of Africa Crisis" situation reports at http://www.unocha.org/crisis/horn-africa-crisis.

[4] USAID, FEWS NET, *Food Assistance Outlook Brief,* August 2011, at http://v4.fews.net/docs/Publications/ FAOB_080811_ext.pdf.

[5] UNOCHA, "Key Figures on Somalia," September 5, 2011.

[6] WFP, "Statement by WFP Executive Director Josette Sheeran on Visit to Mogadishu, Somalia," July 21, 2011; WFP, "Entire Generation At Risk in Horn of Africa, Says WFP Executive Director," July 24, 2011.

[7] Defined broadly as those seeking asylum outside their country of citizenship with protection provided under international law.

[8] A direct result of internal conflict or natural disasters, the internally displaced are also seeking protection but within their state's borders. IDPs do not have the same protection as refugees under international law.

[9] Somali refugees are also in Uganda, Eritrea and Tanzania among other countries. Djibouti, Kenya, and Ethiopia host close to 160,000 other refugees in addition to those from Somalia.

[10] U.N. Office for the Coordination of Humanitarian Affairs. *Horn of Africa Situation Reports.* Various dates.

[11] "UNHCR Issues Urgent Appeal to Kenya to Halt Refoulement of Somali Refugees," UNHCR Posting, November 3, 2010; Amnesty International, *From Life Without Peace to Peace Without Life: The Treatment of Somali Refugees and Asylum-Seekers in Kenya,* AFR 32/015/2010, December 9, 2010. IDPs in Somalia, northern Kenya, and eastern Ethiopia do not have the same rights and protections as refugees under the Refugee Convention because they have not crossed an international border. See also, Human Rights Watch, *You Don't Know Who to Blame: War Crimes in Somalia,* August 2011.

[12] U.N. Office for the Coordination of Humanitarian Affairs. *Horn of Africa Situation Reports.* Various dates.

[13] *Ibid.*

[14] For background information, see CRS Report RL33911, *Somalia: Current Conditions and Prospects for a Lasting Peace,* by Ted Dagne. See also Appendix D in this report.

[15] Freedom House. *Freedom in the World 2011.* January 13, 2011.

[16] Oxfam, "East Africa Food Crisis: Poor Rains, Poor Response," *Oxfam Briefing Note,* July 20, 2011.

[17] See also, CRS Report RL33911, *Somalia: Current Conditions and Prospects for a Lasting Peace,* by Ted Dagne.

[18] Somaliland seceded from the rest of Somalia in 1991, although Somaliland remains unrecognized by the international community. Somaliland is relatively stable and has held a number of free and fair elections over the past decade. In 2010, Ahmed Mohamed Silanyo was elected president when he defeated president Dahir Kahin. The leaders of Puntland, located in northeastern Somalia, declared the region an autonomous state in 1998. Unlike in Somaliland,vPuntland does not seek outright independence from Somalia. Governing authorities in both these regions and in parts of central Somalia are able to provide some social services in areas under their control.

[19] See CRS Report RL34378, *Kenya: Current Conditions and the Challenges Ahead,* by Ted Dagne.

[20] Peter Clottey, "Eritrea Unaffected by Drought, Famine, Says Asmara Official," *VOA News,* July 28, 2011.

[21] African Elections Database. Elections in Djibouti, 2011.

http://www.africanelections.tripod.com.

[22] "Cluster" and "focal point" are terms used by UNOCHA to denote points of coordination and staffing levels: a focal point is smaller than a cluster.

[23] WFP, *Horn of Africa Crisis*, September 15, 2011, http://www.wfp.org/crisis/horn-of-africa.

[24] WFP, *ibid.*

[25] UNOCHA, "Together, we must act to help millions suffering in the Horn of Africa now, and find sustainable ways to build resilience," Press release, September 24, 2011. New pledges were made by Norway, South Korea, Australia, Switzerland, Japan, Ireland, Finland, Italy, Belgium, Russia, Luxembourg, Chile, and Hungary.

[26] Smaller beach ports are also used for aid deliveries.

[27] For further information on Al Shabaab obstructions of aid, see, e.g., U.N. Security Council, *Report of the Monitoring Group on Somalia and Eritrea pursuant to Security Council Resolution 1916 (2010)*, U.N. Document S/2011/433, June 20, 2011; Human Rights Watch, *You Don't Know Who to Blame: War Crimes in Somalia*, August 2011; and UN OCHA's monthly Humanitarian Access reports at http://www.ochaonline.un.org/somalia/SituationReports.

[28] See, e.g., UNOCHA, "OCHA Somalia – Humanitarian Access: Update 01 to 31, March 2010," March 2010, and *Report of the Secretary-General on the Situation in Somalia*, U.N. Document S/2008/178, March 14, 2008. Much of the international humanitarian assistance to the Horn of Africa arrives by sea, and WFP reports that the threat of piracy has made it more expensive to ship assistance to Mogadishu. International naval convoys have escorted food shipments to the region since late 2008. For more information, see CRS Report R40528, *Piracy off the Horn of Africa*, by Lauren Ploch et al.

[29] See U.N. Security Council, *Report of the Monitoring Group on Somalia and Eritrea pursuant to Security Council Resolution 1916 (2010)*, U.N. Document S/2011/433, June 20, 2011.

[30] Al Shabaab raided several U.N. compounds in southern Somalia in July 2009, and issued a decree banning three U.N. agencies (not WFP) from areas under its control in the same month. On February 28, 2010, the Al Shabaab Office for Supervising the Affairs of Foreign Agencies (OSAFA) issued a press statement stating that it had banned all WFP operations inside Somalia.

[31] WFP, Press Release, "Statement by WFP Executive Director Josette Sheeran on Visit to Mogadishu Somalia," July 21, 2011, at http://www.wfp.org/news/news-release/statement-wfp-executive-director-josette-sheeran-visit-mogadishusomalia.

[32] "Somali Rebels Accuse U.N. of Exaggerating Drought Severity, Playing Politics," *Washington Post*, July 21, 2011.

[33] UNOCHA, *Horn of Africa Drought Crisis Situation Report No. 7*, July 29, 2011.

[34] WFP, Horn of Africa Crisis, August 18, 2011, , http://www.wfp.org/crisis/horn-of-africa.

[35] Testimony of Shannon Scribner, Humanitarian Policy Manager for Oxfam America, "Addressing the Humanitarian Emergency in East Africa," before the House Committee on Foreign Affairs, September 8, 2011.

[36] See, e.g., "Insurgents Divert Famine IDPs From Aid," UN IRIN, September 6, 2011.

[37] See, e.g., "Somalian Militant Leader Denounces Reluctant Fighters," Reuters, August 30, 2011; and Council on Foreign Relations, "Al Shabaab and Somalia's Spreading Famine," Interview with Rashid Abdi, International Crisis Group Analyst on the Horn of Africa, August 10, 2011.

[38] The CERF was launched in 2006 to respond to natural disasters and humanitarian emergencies. It is managed by the U.N. Emergency Relief Coordinator and head of UNOCHA. As an international, multilateral funding mechanism, the CERF aims to focus on early

intervention, timely response, and increased capacity and support to underfunded crises. The funds come from voluntary contributions by member states and from the private sector. It is seen by proponents as a way to enable the United Nations to respond more efficiently, effectively, and consistently to humanitarian crises worldwide. Some maintain that U.S. support for this idea is critical to sustaining momentum for donor contributions and continued support for the disaster relief fund. See CERF, Horn of Africa Drought: CERF Support in 2011, September 12, 2011.

[39] UNOCHA, *Horn of Africa Drought Crisis Fact Sheet*, September 20, 2011. See Appendix C.

[40] "Aid Groups Criticize U.S. Response to East Africa Drought," Voice of America, July 23, 2011.

[41] U.N. Security Council, *Report of the Monitoring Group on Somalia and Eritrea pursuant to Security Council Resolution 1916 (2010)*, U.N. Document S/2011/433, p. 56, paragraph 190. June 20, 2011.

[42] UNOCHA, IRIN News, Horn of Africa: "Thinking Outside the Traditional Funding Box," September 1, 2011.

[43] For more information see http://www.usaid.gov/fwd.

[44] USAID, *Horn of Africa – Drought, Fact Sheet #12, Fiscal Year (FY) 2011*, September 15, 2011. http://www.usaid.gov/our_work/humanitarian_assistance/disaster fy2011/hoa_ce_fs10_09-15-2011.pdf

[45] Overseas Development Institute, *Productive Safety Net Program (PSNP), Ethiopia*, 2006, http://www.odi.org.uk/work/projects/details.asp?id=1144&title=productive-safety-net-programme-psnp-ethiopia

[46] USAID, *Feed the Future*, http://www.usaid.gov/our_work/humanitarian_assistance/disaster horn_of_africa/template/fs_sr/fy2011/hoa_ce_fs08_08-18-2011.pdf.

[47] USAID, Feed the Future, Kenya F2010 Implementation Plan, http://www.feedthefuture.gov/documents/ FTF_2010_Implementation_Plan_Kenya.pdf.

[48] "Legal Roadblocks for U.S. Famine Relief to Somalia Creating Humanitarian Crisis," Charity & Security Network, January 27, 2011; Daveed Gartenstein-Ross and Tara Vassefi, "Somalia's Drought, America's Dilemma," *The Atlantic*, July 2011.

[49] Testimony of Jeremy Konyndyk, Mercy Corps Director of Policy and Advocacy, at a Senate Foreign Relations Committee Hearing, "Responding to Drought and Famine in the Horn of Africa," August 3, 2011.

[50] U.S. Department of the Treasury, Office of Foreign Assets Control. "Questions Regarding Private Relief Efforts in Somalia," August 4, 2011; U.S. Department of State, Daily Press Briefing, August 2, 2011.

[51] Eritrea is also subject to a U.N. Security Council arms embargo for its border conflict with Djibouti, efforts to undermine peace and reconciliation in Somalia, and failure to comply with the arms embargo imposed on Somalia (S/RES/1907 (2009), December 23, 2009).

[52] The U.N. Security Council has, since 1992, maintained a nearly comprehensive arms embargo against Somalia, and has frozen its assets in other jurisdictions, blocked travel, and denied arms and related materiel to designated Somali individuals and entities. Citing grave alarm "at the rapid deterioration ... in Somalia and the heavy loss of human life and widespread material damage resulting from the conflict in the country and ... its consequence on stability and peace in the region," the U.N. Security Council requires U.N. member states to impose "a general and complete embargo on all deliveries of weapons and military equipment to Somalia until the Council decides otherwise" (S/RES/733 (1992), January 23, 1992). Subsequent resolutions provided exemptions to these sanctions to facilitate missions

fielded by the United Nations, African Union, and to authorize support for the TFG security forces.

[53] For background information see CRS Report RL33769, *International Crises and Disasters: U.S. Humanitarian Assistance, Budget Trends, and Issues for Congress*, by Rhoda Margesson.

[54] Interaction, "Dear Congress: Use World Humanitarian Day to back foreign laid, news release, August 19, 2011; Bread for the World, "Lives at Stake: Protect Global Food Security Programs," Background Paper, September 2011, no. 216, at http://www.bread.org/what-we-do/resources. Interaction is an umbrella group for 190 U.S.-based Nongovernmental Organizations (NGOs); Bread for the World is a church-based organization that advocates for ending global hunger and malnutrition.

[55] CRS monitors congressional actions on appropriations on a regular basis. See Current Issues in Focus on the CRS web page at
http://www.crs.gov/Pages/clis.aspx?cliid=73&preview=False,
key words agriculture appropriations and state and foreign operations appropriations.

[56] U.N. Security Council, *Report of the Monitoring Group on Somalia pursuant to Security Council Resolution 1853 (2010)*, U.N. Document S/2010/91, March 10, 2010; and U.N. Security Council, *Report of the Monitoring Group on Somalia and Eritrea pursuant to Security Council Resolution 1916 (2010)*, U.N. Document S/2011/433, June 20, 2011.

[57] Associated Press, *AP Exclusive: Food Aid for Starving Somalis Stolen, UN Agency Investigating*, August 15, 2011, http://ca.news.yahoo.com/ap-exclusive-massive-theft World Food Programme, "Statement By The World Food Programme On Humanitarian Operations Providing Food Assistance In Somalia," August 30, 2011.

[58] Ibid.

[59] Heritage Foundation, *Theft of Food Aid in Somalia Should Lead to Congressional Oversight*, Web Memo, September 6, 2011, at
http://www.heritage.org/Research/Reports/2011/09/Theft-of-Food-Aid-in-Somalia-

[60] Testimony of Wouter Schaap, CARE International Somalia Assistant Country Director, at a Senate Foreign Relations Committee Hearing, "Responding to Drought and Famine in the Horn of Africa," August 3, 2011.

[61] CRS interviews and correspondence with NGO representatives in Washington, DC, September 2011.

[62] Relief Web is a good source of information, although the accuracy is not guaranteed. See http://www.reliefweb.int. Obtaining an exact up-to-date record of all international contributions in response to an ongoing disaster is often not possible—in part because some assistance is not reported to governments or coordinating agencies—and in part because of the delay in their recording.

[63] U.N. document S/RES/2010 (2011), September 30, 2011.

In: Humanitarian Crisis and Response ...   ISBN: 978-1-61942-540-8
Editors: C.J. Newsome and H.I. Herron © 2012 Nova Science Publishers, Inc.

Chapter 2

WRITTEN TESTIMONY OF NANCY E. LINDBORG, ASSISTANT ADMINISTRATOR, BUREAU FOR DEMOCRACY, CONFLICT, AND HUMANITARIAN ASSISTANCE, UNITED STATES AGENCY FOR INTERNATIONAL DEVELOPMENT, BEFORE THE COMMITTEE ON FOREIGN RELATIONS, SUBCOMMITTEE ON AFRICAN AFFAIRS, UNITED STATES SENATE, DROUGHT AND FAMINE IN THE HORN OF AFRICA, AUGUST 4, 2011

Chairman Coons, Ranking Member Isakson, and distinguished members of the Committee, thank you for this opportunity to testify before you today on the humanitarian crisis in the Horn of Africa. Your attention and concern is critical, as the situation continues to deteriorate daily, with millions of individuals affected.

In scale and severity, the current drought in the Horn of Africa is the worst in 60 years and, according to the UN Office of the Coordination for Humanitarian Affairs, it is now affecting an estimated 12.4 million people in Somalia, Kenya, Ethiopia, and Djibouti. It is both a humanitarian and a security crisis, as famine has been declared in the difficult to access areas of

Somalia and refugees are pouring across the borders into already drought-stressed areas of Kenya and Ethiopia.

I will discuss today the current situation, our immediate response, the challenges we face, and our long term plans to address the chronic food insecurity in the Horn of Africa.

CURRENT SITUATION

The Horn of Africa is experiencing the lowest rains in 60 years, in a region long plagued by cyclical drought. However, what used to be a ten year drought cycle is now occurring every other year and is combined with rising food prices and a 20 year conflict in Somalia.

Twenty five years ago, USAID invested in the Famine Early Warning System, or FEWSNET, precisely because of the recurring droughts in the region. FEWSNET, along with the UN Food and Agriculture Organization's Food Security and Nutrition Analysis Unit (FSNAU), maintains a strong presence in the Horn and enables the humanitarian community to identify conditions based on an extensive analysis of historical and current rainfall, cropping patterns, livestock health, market prices and malnutrition rates. USAID is the largest supporter of these vital early warning systems, and the entire international humanitarian and donor community relies on their information to provide appropriate assistance to those who need it most and to target assistance that might be needed in the future.

In Ethiopia and Kenya, the situation is grave but we do not expect it to deteriorate into famine. Both countries have large areas of arid lands populated primarily by pastoralists. Ethiopia has declared 4.8 million in need of urgent assistance, and in Kenya, 3.7 million are at risk. USAID has worked extensively in both countries, in partnership with international donors and local governments; to increase the resilience and food security of communities in these drought affected areas. We have focused better on early warning systems, ongoing safety-net and community protection programs, and increased productivity in arid lands and pastoralist livelihoods.

For example, in partnership with the Ethiopian government, the World Bank and other donors, the United States supported the Ethiopian Productive Safety Net program, which has effectively removed approximately 7.6 million people from the emergency caseload. In the drought of 2002-3, the Government of Ethiopia stated that 13.2 million people in Ethiopia were drought-affected and in need of emergency assistance. By contrast, that number to date is 4.8 million. The needs in these countries are still serious and require sustained focus and attention, but the results of preparedness and development investments are having a positive impact.

In Somalia, however, the situation is stark. Consecutive seasons of failed or poor rainfall, coupled with two decades of conflict and lack of governance, have resulted in rising food prices, livestock mortality, crop failure, denial of reliable humanitarian access by al-Shabaab, and consequent severe malnutrition and massive population displacement. The U.N. estimates that a total of 3.2 million people in Somalia now require immediate, life-saving humanitarian assistance. Of those in urgent need, 2.8 million people reside in southern Somalia. On July 20, the U.N. declared a famine in two regions of Somalia: Lower Shabelle Region and areas of Bakool Region in southern Somalia. A famine determination is never made lightly and reflects the truly dire circumstances facing the people of southern Somalia. Based on nutrition and mortality surveys verified by the Centers for Disease Control and Prevention (CDC), we estimate that more than 29,000 children under five _ nearly four percent of children -- have died in the last 90 days in southern Somalia.

Somalis are leaving the south in great numbers, either for the more stable areas in the north or into neighboring countries _ in all cases adding great strain to already drought-stressed environments. More specifically, 1.5 million internally displaced Somalis are concentrated in Mogadishu and the regions of Lower Shabelle and Galgaduud, with increasing numbers in Puntland and Somaliland. In May, I traveled to Hargeysa, in the semi-autonomous region of Somaliland, where I met with President Sulanyo, as well as UN and local and international nongovernmental organizations. They noted rising concerns about the numbers of internally displaced persons who are now arriving in their cities, ill-equipped to meet the needs of a rising population. Farmers and pastoralists, with no remaining assets, are swelling the outskirts of cities throughout northern Somalia, including many youth with no evident future.

The refugees who cross into Ethiopia and Kenya describe a grueling trip, often on foot for three to four or more weeks. My colleague, Deputy Assistant Secretary Reuben Brigety, will describe in more detail the deeply distressing stories of families arriving in refugee camps in near-death shape. Tragically, we also know that in these crisis situations, those who leave are the ones with the strength and resources to do so. The weakest and most vulnerable are often left behind.

CURRENT U.S. GOVERNMENT ASSISTANCE TO THE HORN DROUGHT AND FAMINE

FEWSNET warned us of the increased probabilities of drought in August 2010. Because of these early warnings, USAID began prepositioning additional emergency relief supplies and food aid in the region last fall, stockpiling food aid supplies in Djibouti, South Africa and Kenya. As a result, the U.S. Government was able to help jump-start relief efforts and is now reaching more than 4.6 million in need throughout the Horn and providing approximately $459 million in humanitarian assistance to date (in FY 2011). U.S. assistance provides critically needed food aid, treatment for severely malnourished children, health care, clean water, proper sanitation, and hygiene education and supplies. The United States is providing approximately $217 million in Ethiopia, $156 million in Kenya, $80 million in Somalia, and $6 million in Djibouti. Since the drought began, for example, USAID assisted the Government of Ethiopia to vaccinate nearly 300,000 livestock, critical for the survival of 25,000 households.

Our strategy is focused on providing emergency assistance for those most at-risk, while also continuing to build greater food security and resilience in the drought-affected communities of Kenya, Ethiopia and northern parts of Somalia so they can better withstand future droughts and shocks.

We have been responding since last fall with prepositioning of supplies and increasing programs. Last spring, we created a Horn of Africa Drought Task Force in Nairobi, and on July 6, USAID activated a regional Disaster Assistance Response Team (DART) in Nairobi, Kenya, and Addis Ababa, Ethiopia, to monitor regional drought conditions, identify anticipated response needs, and coordinate response activities with other donors. USAID also stood up a Response Management Team in Washington, D.C., to support the DART and coordinate U.S. Government humanitarian efforts. The DART continues to conduct assessments in the field to evaluate ongoing humanitarian needs and coordinates daily with other major donors to ensure a multilateral response.

In FY 2011 to date, USAID has provided more than 360,200 metric tons (MT) of Title II food relief and emergency food assistance through the U.N. World Food Program (WFP) and nongovernmental organizations for drought- and conflict-affected populations in Djibouti, Ethiopia, Kenya, and Somalia— supporting approximately 10.7 million people.

Given the urgency of reaching the people in southern Somalia, we have a special focus on aggressively working to abate the potential for mass starvation. We have learned from the Somalia drought of 1992 that disease was a leading cause of death for children under five, so we are stressing a multi-sector response with a focus on three key areas: availability of food, access to food, and integrated public health interventions—including therapeutic feeding focused on the children under five, vaccinations, and access to clean water and sanitation.

Based on FEWSNET data, we do not expect a significant harvest in the south for another six months. The next potential rains are in September or October in the south, and even if there are good rains, we could experience another wave of mortality due to water-borne disease and livestock death.

We are working closely with other donors and U.N. and NGO partners to mount an effective response to save lives. We have three key challenges: time, access and scale. As noted earlier, time is not on our side. Unfortunately, the situation is going to worsen before it gets better. However, we know we have a small window over the next six weeks in which to provide life-saving assistance to prevent additional and potential significant deaths from occurring. The fear is that without immediate and significant assistance, famine conditions will spread from the two regions in southern Somalia to encompass the entire eight regions of the south with several hundred thousand additional deaths.

Access remains difficult in the worst affected areas of southern Somalia. The World Food Program and most international NGOs had suspended operations in the south due to deteriorating security and bans imposed by al-Shabaab. Since 2008, WFP has lost 14 staff members in attacks. However, we are in lockstep with other donors and the humanitarian community in our determination to test aggressively all options for delivering assistance in previously inaccessible areas to the people in southern Somalia.

Finally, the scale of this emergency outstrips the resources currently offered by the international community to meet the needs. We are working to encourage the broader international community to step forward with additional assistance as we seek to address this sobering challenge.

Looking Ahead: Feed the Future

We can't stop drought from happening, but we can strengthen communities and their ability to prepare for and withstand these kinds of natural calamities. President Obama's Feed the Future initiative(FTF) is focused precisely on addressing these root causes of hunger and under nutrition. It seeks to increase longer term resilience among vulnerable populations by increasing the commercial availability and accessibility of staple foods, reducing trade and transport barriers that impede the movement and sale of livestock and staple foods, harnessing science and technology to assist populations in increasing crop yields, and supporting national and regional efforts to reduce years of marginalization of certain populations. USAID is focusing its investments, both geographically and programmatically, to have the greatest sustainable impacts on reducing hunger and poverty. By linking vulnerable populations to market opportunities in more productive areas, our efforts are helping increase labor opportunities and strengthen value chains.

In the Somali, Oromiya and Afar National regional States of Ethiopia for example, FTF investments are helping vulnerable pastoralists and ex-pastoralists and Afar to improve their incomes and increase their ability to survive climate and economic shocks. USAID is helping these pastoralists to improve the health of their animals through strengthening community veterinary services and accessing affordable vaccinations and other medicine. In addition, we are working to help pastoralists earn more money from their animals by linking them to markets where they can sell their animals for a significant profit. We help producers organize into marketing cooperatives and access much needed credit, improve their business skills and provide them access to market information. Stronger linkages between traders, feed lot operator, processors and exporters also help to expand livestock trade and provide better access to lucrative markets in the region.

We are seeing with this drought the critical and positive impact of investing in the future. When countries have the governance structures, the policies and productive capacity to withstand drought and when communities have the resilience to withstand the inevitable shocks of droughts and crisis, the need for large-scale international emergency assistance is diminished. Even as we focus on the heart-breaking tragedy of Somalia, we are also committed to helping to build sustainable futures where communities feed themselves.

Thank you, Mr. Chairman and Members of the Committee.

In: Humanitarian Crisis and Response ...   ISBN: 978-1-61942-540-8
Editors: C.J. Newsome and H.I. Herron © 2012 Nova Science Publishers, Inc.

Chapter 3

TESTIMONY, PRINCIPAL DEPUTY ASSISTANT SECRETARY DON YAMAMOTO, BUREAU OF AFRICAN AFFAIRS, UNITED STATES DEPARTMENT OF STATE, BEFORE THE SENATE FOREIGN RELATIONS, SUBCOMMITTEE ON AFRICAN AFFAIRS, "RESPONDING TO DROUGHT AND FAMINE IN THE HORN OF AFRICA", WEDNESDAY, AUGUST, 3, 2011

Good morning, Chairman Coons, Ranking Member Isakson, and members of the Committee. Thank you for holding this hearing on the drought and famine in the Horn of Africa. We share your grave concern about the ongoing humanitarian crisis in the Horn of Africa. The eastern Horn of Africa is currently experiencing one of the worst droughts since the 1950s. More than 12 million people—mainly in Ethiopia, Kenya, and Somalia—are severely affected and in need of humanitarian assistance. In Somalia, drought conditions have exacerbated a complex emergency that has continued since 1991. The information coming out of the Horn of Africa, especially the dire situation of refugees from Somalia, is devastating. In cooperation with our international and regional partners, we will continue to work to address this humanitarian crisis while continuing to support long-term political and food security in the region.

Somalia is at the center of the crisis, but the crisis is affecting the entire Horn of Africa. Ethiopia has issued an appeal indicating 4.5 million Ethiopians need food assistance. In Kenya, the government and a consortium of NGOs have placed 10 districts in the north and east under alert for increased food insecurity and malnutrition. The crisis has hit hardest in Somalia, where failed or poor rains combined with conflict have left 3.7 million people in need of immediate, lifesaving assistance. Two areas of southern Somalia, the Lower Shabelle Region and areas of the Bakool region, are currently facing famine conditions, and the remaining regions of southern Somalia are projected to meet the threshold for famine unless humanitarian assistance is significantly increased.

The number of refugees and internally displaced persons (IDPs) across the region has increased the challenges of drought response. There are approximately 620,000 Somali refugees in the eastern Horn region, according the UN High Commissioner for Refugees (UNHCR), with 200,000 of these fleeing in the past year alone. Reports from inside Somalia indicate the combined arrival rate of 2,000 new refugees per day in Ethiopia and Kenya could rise dramatically as the situation in Somalia grows increasingly desperate. The current flows threaten to overwhelm the existing refugee assistance structure in Kenya and Ethiopia. Moreover, there are reports of over 400,000 IDPs in Mogadishu alone.

A large-scale multi-donor intervention—my colleagues will go into greater depth on this—is underway to prevent the further decline of an already dire situation, but there will be no quick fix. The United States is one of the largest donors of emergency assistance to the region, helping more than 4.5 million of those in need in Ethiopia, Kenya, Somalia, and Djibouti and providing nearly $459 million in humanitarian assistance to date. Our assistance includes food, treatment for severely malnourished people, health care, clean water, proper sanitation, and hygiene education and supplies. Our assistance also includes $69 million for refugee assistance in Kenya, Ethiopia, and Djibouti. The U.S. government has previously supported the expansion of the Dadaab camps, and we understand that the Government of Kenya has agreed to allow new refugees to begin occupying the new areas. Our Embassy in Nairobi is actively engaged with the Kenyans to ensure the best possible emergency response. I know my colleagues Principal Deputy Assistant Secretary Reuben Brigety and Assistant Administrator Nancy Lindborg will go into greater detail about these conditions in their testimony; I would like to turn now to the political complications of the drought in Somalia.

The response to the drought has been complicated by the continuing instability in Somalia—especially due to the actions of al-Shabaab. Those most seriously affected by the current drought are the more than two million Somalis trapped in al-Shabaab-controlled areas in south central Somalia. Since January 2010, al-Shabaab has largely prohibited international humanitarian workers and organizations from operating in the areas it controls. Al-Shabaab's continued refusal to grant humanitarian access has prevented the international community from responding to the drought in south central Somalia, which precipitated the famine we are seeing now. The United States is pressing all parties to immediately restore unimpeded humanitarian access to all parts of Somalia.

During the last week of July, major fighting began again in Mogadishu between the African Union Mission in Somalia (AMISOM) and the Transitional Federal Government (TFG) forces against al-Shabaab and its affiliates. With more than 400,000 IDPs now residing in and around Mogadishu, this renewed fighting is an area of concern. We are confident that AMISOM and the TFG understand the threat this fighting places on the civilian population and call on all parties to do everything in their power to protect civilians, particularly those displaced due to recent famine and drought conditions. We continue to support AMISOM and the TFG in their efforts to bring stability to Mogadishu in the face of continuing threats from al-Shabaab.

Al-Shabaab is a U.S.-designated Foreign Terrorist Organization and has also been sanctioned by the United Nations for its role in threatening the peace, security, and stability of Somalia including disrupting the Djibouti Peace Process; and for obstructing humanitarian assistance into Somalia. As we seek to take advantage of any current openings to expand aid distribution, we are also working with our partners in the international community to counter al-Shabaab's ability to threaten our interests or continue to hold the Somali people hostage. At the same time, we are taking the necessary steps to support the flow of urgently needed humanitarian aid to those who need it in south central Somalia while working to minimize any risk of diversion to al-Shabaab. We have worked closely with the Department of Treasury to ensure that aid workers—who are partnering with the U.S. Government to help save lives under difficult and dangerous conditions—are not in conflict with U.S. laws and regulations. To be clear, however, the U.S. sanctions against al-Shabaab do not and never have prohibited the delivery of assistance to Somalia, including to those areas under the de facto control of alShabaab. The presence of Al-Shabaab means that U.S. persons must adhere to U.S. legal requirements in the course of providing assistance in Somalia.

In the long term, regional security in the Horn of Africa requires political stability in Somalia. The United States already has in place a long-term process to stabilize Somalia. Last year we announced the Dual Track approach to broaden our efforts by taking into account the complex nature of Somali society and politics, as well as to be more flexible and adaptable in our engagement. On Track One, we continue support for the Djibouti Peace Process, the TFG, and AMISOM as a first line of effort to stabilize Somalia and expel al-Shabaab from Mogadishu. Since 2007, the United States has supported stabilization efforts by obligating approximately $258 million to support AMISOM's training and logistical needs, as well as approximately $85 million to support and build the capacity of TFG forces. Recent security advances by AMISOM and the TFG in Mogadishu have taken back significant portions of the city from al-Shabaab control.

On Track Two, we are deepening our engagement with the regional governments of Somaliland and Puntland, as well as with local and regional administrations throughout South Central Somalia who are opposed to al-Shabaab, but who are not affiliated with the TFG. In FY 11, the United States plans to provide approximately $21 million to support development efforts in support of the Dual Track policy. We are reviewing how best to adapt our travel policy for Somalia to execute our Dual Track approach most effectively without compromising on our obligation to protect the security of U.S. personnel when they travel inside Somalia. Our long-term efforts will continue to focus on security, governance, and humanitarian and development assistance.

In addition to working towards political stability in Somalia, the U.S. government is also focusing its efforts to help provide long-term food security in the eastern Horn of Africa region. We recognize that emergency assistance alone cannot solve the underlying long-term problems in the region. That is why President Obama's innovative and forward-looking Feed the Future initiative is so critical. Feed the Future is already at work in the region with local, regional, and multilateral partners improving agricultural production, improving markets, building infrastructure, bringing innovation, and addressing the entire value chain—from seed to market.

As I noted when I began, we are extremely concerned about the drought and famine in the Horn of Africa. We are working hard with our interagency and international partners to deliver quickly the life-saving short-term relief critical to those suffering its effects. U.S. government and U.S.-funded assistance has prevented the loss of millions of lives. We recognize that both the food security problem in the region and the political instability problem in

Somalia are linked, and that both demand long-term solutions. Our Dual Track approach to Somalia provides an effective mechanism for us to grapple with the challenges of political stability in Somalia. Our Feed the Future initiative will help create food security in the eastern Horn of Africa region. The United States will continue to monitor and respond to the humanitarian crisis and work with host governments on long-term solutions. Thank you, Mr. Chairman. I welcome your questions.

In: Humanitarian Crisis and Response ...   ISBN: 978-1-61942-540-8
Editors: C.J. Newsome and H.I. Herron © 2012 Nova Science Publishers, Inc.

Chapter 4

WRITTEN TESTIMONY OF REUBEN E. BRIGETY, II, DEPUTY ASSISTANT SECRETARY, BUREAU FOR POPULATION, REFUGEES, AND MIGRATION, UNITED STATES DEPARTMENT OF STATE, BEFORE THE COMMITTEE ON FOREIGN RELATIONS, SUBCOMMITTEE ON AFRICAN AFFAIRS, UNITED STATES SENATE, DROUGHT AND FAMINE IN THE HORN OF AFRICA, AUGUST 3, 2011

Chairman Coons, Ranking Member Isakson, and distinguished members of the Committee, thank you for this opportunity to testify before you today on the humanitarian crisis in the Horn of Africa. We appreciate the support and attention Congress has given to this crisis in the midst of so many other issues you have been grappling with this summer.

I will discuss today the current situation facing refugees, our immediate response, the challenges we face in meeting their needs as more famine survivors reach the borders of Kenya, Ethiopia, and Djibouti, and our plans to work with the world community to meet those challenges and save as many lives as we possibly can in the coming months ahead.

REFUGEE OVERVIEW

I travelled to Ethiopia and Kenya in July to evaluate the emerging refugee crisis in the region where hundreds of thousands of Somalis have fled drought and famine in Somalia. During my trip, I visited refugee camps in each country along with representatives from donor countries, met with senior government officials, talked with officials from UN agencies and non-governmental organizations, and spoke with refugees. It was clear that this is developing into the worst humanitarian emergency that the region has seen in a generation, at least since the great famine of 1991-1992. We now must confront a refugee emergency within a protracted refugee situation. Years of hard work by the host governments and their international partners to address just the basic needs within established camps quickly are being overshadowed by the need to add new border-crossing facilities, new camps, and emergency services.

Both Ethiopia and Kenya are receiving record inflows of refugees from Somalia, and in both countries refugees are arriving in appalling physical health. Every refugee family with whom I spoke in both Ethiopia and Kenya said that they had walked for days from Somalia with virtually no food and water. Brief visits to the health clinics in the refugee camps revealed dozens of malnourished children, so emaciated and weak that they appeared to the untrained eye to be close to death. Among new arrivals in the refugee camps in Ethiopia, we are seeing up to 50% global acute malnutrition– reflecting the even more grim state of affairs for children inside Somalia. Camps in Ethiopia and Kenya are strained far beyond capacity in every way – with regard to space, staff, food, and essential services – trying to cope with the record influx of refugees, which continues unabated.

Somalis represent the largest refugee population in Africa. According to UNHCR, Somalia's neighbors in the eastern Horn of Africa now host more than 620,000 Somali refugees. Some 159,000 Somalis have sought refuge in Ethiopia; over 75,000 have arrived just since January 2011. Kenya hosts more than 448,000 Somali refugees with nearly 100,000 since the beginning of the year. Even Djibouti has seen an almost twenty percent increase in the number of refugees since the beginning of the year. We commend the governments of Kenya, Djibouti, and Ethiopia for their generous support for refugee populations in the region, even as they themselves are currently struggling with a drought that may be the worst in 60 years.

While the current crisis is taxing an already stressed system, I am confident governments of Kenya, Ethiopia, Djibouti, and their international partners, including the U.S., have the ability to confront this crisis head on and will be able to find new solutions to address the needs not only within the camps but also for those within Somalia. Let me give you just two examples of what I saw during my trip and how we are responding to those in need.

THE LONG JOURNEY OF THE SURVIVORS

First, the U.S. and our regional and international partners have helped ramp up emergency assistance. I traveled to the refugee camp complex at Dolo Ado on the Ethiopian-Somali border accompanied by US Ambassador to Ethiopia Donald Booth, USAID Deputy Administrator Don Steinberg, Ethiopian government officials, UNHCR's Ethiopia Country Representative, and senior representatives from several embassies, including Australia, the United Kingdom, Canada, Sweden, and the European Union. As we wandered through the refugee camp, talking with people who had been there for several days or who had just crossed the border a few hours earlier, we heard versions of the same story over and over again.

One man I met had come all the way from Mogadishu, traveling for nine days with his wife and six children with very little to eat along the way. I talked with him as he sat on the hospital cot of his youngest child -- a three-year-old girl I'll call Aisha. As we spoke, Aisha never stopped moaning. She could not get comfortable amidst the heat and flies as her tiny bones threatened to pierce her paper-thin skin. We saw many families in the same desperate situation during a separate visit to Dadaab refugee camp in Kenya. In Dadaab, I spoke to one mother who had carried her polio-stricken seven-year-old daughter on her back for nine days with little food and water as her other six children trailed behind.

It was clear that a number of recent interventions – such as the provision of hot meals at the transit center or the establishment of blanket feeding programs – are vital steps needed beyond just basic camp services to assist those making this heartbreaking journey. I commend Antonio Guterres, the UN High Commissioner for Refugees, for finding ways to add these additional programs around Dolo Ado after he himself visited the area and found ways to move resources and personnel into place more quickly. Still more is needed and we in the international community cannot slacken our efforts.

CURRENT U.S. GOVERNMENT
ASSISTANCE TO REFUGEES

Second, the U.S. has increased overall refugee assistance throughout the region. The U.S. has long been a partner to the governments and people of the Horn of Africa as they host hundreds of thousands of Somali refugees, providing approximately $459 million in humanitarian assistance this fiscal year to help those in need. This funding supports refugees, internally displaced persons (IDPs), and other drought affected populations, and helps build resiliency and food security beyond the immediate crisis. Out of this overall funding, the U.S. is providing approximately $69 million, specifically for refugee assistance in the region through the Department of State's Population, Refugees, and Migration bureau.

Maintaining access to safe asylum for Somalis in neighboring countries is critical to saving lives. The U.S. has previously supported the expansion of the Dadaab camps and UNHCR is now moving refugees into the new space following the government of Kenya's agreement to allow the opening of the new site. We are also urging Kenya to quickly open more reception center capacity so that incoming refugees can be properly screened and registered. We will continue to support the Horn countries' efforts to provide asylum to vulnerable Somalis, including through our support for the Office of the UN High Commissioner for Refugees, the World Food Program, and other international organizations and NGOs working in the region.

Representatives from other donor countries who accompanied me were moved by the gravity of the situation and said they would work with their governments to support the efforts of aid groups. Rigorous and sustained diplomacy will be required both in the region and with other donor capitals to ensure that the international community and host countries take necessary measures to save lives in the coming months. We need to ensure that insecurity from Somalia does not spill over into the neighboring countries.

We are also committed to addressing the humanitarian needs inside Somalia so that lives are saved and fewer people need to flee to the neighboring countries. There is an immediate need to reach vulnerable populations inside Somalia who may be unable to travel long distances to seek life-saving assistance. Ideally drought victims would not have to leave their homes in order to receive life-saving assistance, but in conflicted Somalia, that is not currently possible in all instances.

That brings us to the security situation. Al-Shabaab's activities have clearly made the current situation much worse. We expect the situation in Somalia to continue to decline, especially in southern Somalia where the UN has declared famine in two regions to date and where conditions continue to worsen. The international community is calling on al-Shabaab to allow unimpeded assistance in these areas of Somalia, including allowing aid groups access to the direst areas to directly assist those in greatest need.

There is not a single solution – to this regional crisis. We are working to tackle it through a variety of mechanisms and responses, including addressing the underlying causes, as noted by my colleague, Assistant Administrator Lindborg.

Thank you, Mr. Chairman and Members of the Committee.

In: Humanitarian Crisis and Response ...   ISBN: 978-1-61942-540-8
Editors: C.J. Newsome and H.I. Herron © 2012 Nova Science Publishers, Inc.

Chapter 5

STATEMENT OF JEREMY KONYNDYK, DIRECTOR OF POLICY AND ADVOCACY, MERCY CORPS, UNITED STATES SENATE COMMITTEE ON FOREIGN RELATIONS, SUBCOMMITTEE ON AFRICA, HEARING ON: *RESPONDING TO DROUGHT AND FAMINE IN THE HORN OF AFRICA*, AUGUST 3, 2011

Chairman Coons,
Ranking Member Isakson:

Thank you for inviting me to testify before the Sub-Committee today on the critically important issue of drought and famine in the Horn of Africa. I am here today in my capacity as Director of Policy and Advocacy for Mercy Corps, a global relief and development organization that responds to disasters and supports community development in more than forty countries around the world. Mercy Corps has worked in the Horn for many years, and we currently manage relief and development programs in the three countries most affected by the drought: Kenya, Ethiopia, and Somalia. In these countries we have hundreds of staff providing assistance to 900,000 drought victims. We are working in many of the areas most affected by the drought: North and Central Somalia, Eastern Ethiopia, and Northeastern Kenya. In these regions we are pursuing a range of drought-focused interventions, including providing access to water; supporting livelihoods so that people can afford to feed themselves and protect their livestock; aiding communities to better manage the scarce water resources that they have; and providing supplemental nutrition to at-risk children and mothers. We are undertaking these programs with the generous support of public and private donors, including the important contributions of the US Agency for International Development.

With 12.4 million people across the Horn in already in a state of humanitarian crisis – a figure that has increased by three million in just the past month – this emergency threatens to become the worst humanitarian catastrophe of the past several decades. While most attention has focused on Somalia, this is truly a regional emergency: people in Kenya, Ethiopia, and Djibouti all face major shortfalls in access to food and water as well. The situation within southern Somalia is catastrophic, with death rates in the worst-affected regions, particularly among children, up to triple the threshold for declaring a famine and levels of malnutrition that are also well beyond the famine threshold.[1] The situation in the rest of the region is less catastrophic, but still extremely dire. Across Kenya, Ethiopia, and central Somalia, Mercy Corps teams are seeing people's livelihoods collapse in real time, pushing the affected populations closer and closer to calamity. The situation, while already desperate, promises to worsen in coming months as remaining water and food stocks are further depleted. The international response, though it has accelerated in recent weeks, remains inadequate. In the hardest-hit region, southern Somalia, security obstacles continue to impede the delivery of assistance and international legal restrictions have further compounded the challenges of operating there. Without swift action on all fronts, the drought will have devastating human and regional impacts that will be impossible to roll back.

HOW IS THIS CRISIS DIFFERENT?

While drought is common in the Horn of Africa, the current situation is far graver than the normal cycles of drought that occasionally hit the region. Several factors contribute to this. First is the rainfall over the past year, which in most areas is among the lowest ever recorded. The region has two main rainy seasons per year, one in the fall and one in the late spring to early summer. Over the past year, both largely failed, leaving the driest conditions that most parts of the Horn have seen in 60 years. Seven districts across swaths of northeastern Kenya and southern Ethiopia have recorded the driest season since 1950.[2] The broad area across which the rains failed is also unique: a typical drought in the region would be less uniform, enabling people to temporarily relocate to other areas to find water. This time, the broad coverage of the drought has meant that people's normal "backup" locations are themselves in a state of drought. Finally, this drought comes on the heels of another serious regional drought in 2008 which, though less severe than the current situation, left elevated vulnerability across the region.

The result has been a progressive erosion of the capacity of people in the region to cope with economic and climatic shocks. Most rural and nomadic populations in the Horn depend on livestock herding or small-scale agriculture to support themselves. Both forms of livelihood are heavily dependent on water and vulnerable to drought. In a milder drought, people would rely on a variety of "coping mechanisms" to see themselves through: shifting herds to different areas in search of alternate water sources; selling off land holdings or parts of their herds to generate extra income; substituting for less expensive foods; reducing meals; and cutting back on household expenses.

The severity of the current drought, coming on the heels of the 2008 drought, has exhausted these coping mechanisms and left people with no income and few options. The failure of the rains across the region has meant that there are few areas where livestock can be shifted to find alternate water sources. Those that exist are quickly depleted by the increased pressure. Selling livestock at market generates little to no income because the condition of most livestock is so poor that they can fetch little money. Livestock are a form of both income and savings for people in the region; as huge numbers of livestock have died off they have wiped out the savings and income potential of innumerable families. The poor rains have led to widespread crop failures across the region, greatly reducing the local supply of food both at a household level and in regional markets. The prices of locally produced staples accordingly reached record highs in June in most markets throughout the eastern Horn. [3] In some parts of Somalia, prices of staple cereals like white maize have increased by as much as 350 percent above last year.[4] This massive inflation has quickly wiped out what scant savings people may have. These factors, taken together, can quickly lead to a complete collapse in peoples' ability to feed themselves. With their livestock assets depleted or deceased, no yield from their own agriculture, their savings spent, their land sold, and food in the market priced beyond reach, people find themselves without options. Aid or migration become their only possibilities for survival.

In southern Somalia, as we are now vividly seeing, this process has fully run its course. The result is some of the most devastating human suffering that aid professionals have ever seen. The desperation and destitution of those who have fled to Kenya, central Somalia, and Ethiopia has been well-documented: "roads of death" on which mothers are forced to leave behind the children who die en route; cases of advanced malnutrition so severe that those lucky enough to obtain treatment still have only a 40% chance of survival[5]; a torrent of refugees and internally displaced persons so large that camps and reception centers have been quickly overwhelmed. As disturbing as the refugee situation is, there are many more within Somalia who are too poor or too weak to even make the journey out. The slowdown in refugee arrival numbers in Ethiopia and Kenya over the past week may indicate, ominously, that the bulk of those who were capable of leaving have now done so. The numbers from FEWSNET suggest that those who remain in the south are now dying in astronomically large numbers. Child mortality in every district of southern Somalia now surpasses famine levels. In the worst-hit areas, children under five are dying at a rate five times the famine threshold[6]. At this rate more than a tenth of the under-five population in these areas is being wiped out every two months. Tens of thousands of people are estimated to have already died, a number that could reach into the hundreds of thousands if the situation continues to deteriorate as expected.

In Kenya, Central Somalia, and Ethiopia, the wider availability of aid and the existence of government safety net programs have slowed the process of livelihood collapse. But existing aid flows are not keeping up with the growing challenges, and safety net programs are not built to handle such massive levels of need. UNICEF estimates that over a quarter of the more than two million acutely malnourished children across the drought-affected Horn are at risk of death.[7] The humanitarian needs in Kenya and Ethiopia are important to address in their own right, but they have added significance given the growing refugee populations in both countries. It is well-established that provision of aid to refugees can provoke resentment and backlash from host communities, ultimately endangering the refugees, if the needs of those host communities are not also met.

Mercy Corps teams in Ethiopia and Kenya report mounting needs that are approaching critical levels in many areas. In Kenya, while most international attention has focused on the Dadaab refugee camp, the Kenyan population in the northeast of the country is entering a critical phase. The current dry spell is expected to last through at least October and food insecurity will get worse over the next few months.[8] Livestock are dying in large numbers due to lack of water, and this crop cycle will be a near-total failure in many parts of the country due to the drought.[9] The situation is so desperate that our assessments have found instances of herders braving security challenges to take their remaining livestock into riverine parts of Somalia to attempt to water them there. This has led to a phenomenon of "drought widows" – women whose husbands have left to seek water for their livestock, leaving their families behind indefinitely. Malnutrition rates have been rising, and an estimated 40 percent of farming households in some districts are now skipping meals.[10] Our teams expect to begin seeing elevated mortality rates in the very near future if swift action is not taken. In Ethiopia we are seeing a parallel situation. Recently-completed assessments by Mercy Corps in eastern Ethiopia revealed that the drought is already having a massive impact on the population. In some areas that we visited, entire villages were empty – their inhabitants forced to move as the drought devastated their ability to support and feed themselves. Dead cattle litter the landscape, and along one 40-kilometer stretch of road we visited not a single bit of foliage was visible. Many families have been reduced to eating one meal per day. Ethiopian colleagues who have been living and working in the region for decades have told us that they have never before seen anything like this.

SCALING UP THE RESPONSE

The international community's response to the drought has been substantial, but nowhere near adequate. The United Nations estimates that nearly $2.5 billion will be required to meet the region's needs this year.[11] International contributions for humanitarian response, currently around $1.3 billion, are well below this target, and indeed are running well behind the levels contributed just three years ago, when a lesser drought gripped the region. Compared to other major disaster such as the Haiti earthquake or the Indian Ocean Tsunami, the drought crisis in the Horn is receiving a fraction of the attention and support that was committed to those emergencies. This reflects the paradox that aid agencies often face with slow-onset disasters: compared to more-telegenic natural disasters, in which most of the death and injury occur instantaneously, in slow onset disasters we can potentially save far, far more of the threatened lives. Yet we typically have a much harder time mobilizing the resources required to do so. We are working hard to convey to the public in the US and other donor states that their support is badly needed. However, private contributions for this emergency are many times lower than the generous levels contributed after other major disasters.

On the US side, the work of the government's emergency responders in USAID's Office of Foreign Disaster Assistance (OFDA) and Office of Food for Peace (FFP), as well as the State Department's Bureau of Population, Refugees, and Migration (PRM) has been exemplary. These offices possess a high level of expertise and professionalism, and they have focused on this crisis with great seriousness and energy. Their response is to be commended. But they will need ample resources well into the next fiscal year if they are to sustain an aggressive response to this emergency.

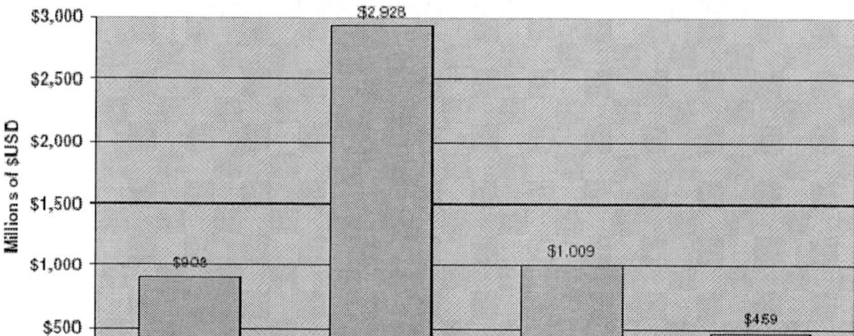

Sources: GAO: USAID Tsunami Signature Reconstruction Efforts in Indonesia and Sri Lanka Exceed Initial Cost and Schedule Estimates, Face Further Risk (February 2007);

GAO: Haiti Reconstruction - U.S. Efforts Have Begun, Expanded Oversight Still to be Implemented (May 2011); USAID Fact Sheet #10: Horn of Africa Complex Emergency (October 31, 2008); USAID Fact Sheet #4: Horn of Africa Drought (July 28, 2011)

US contributions to the Horn of Africa are down significantly relative to 2008. The Bush Administration's humanitarian contributions that year topped one billion dollars region-wide, while this year the US has contributed less than half that amount. [12] To put this in perspective, the US contribution towards the drought this year amounts to roughly one-sixth of the amount that Congress appropriated for the Haiti response in the 2010 supplemental; this despite the fact that the population at risk in the Horn is greater than the entire population of Haiti. US support to this drought also lags far behind US contributions to other major crises, as the chart below demonstrates.

In Somalia specifically, US support dropped off drastically from 2008 to 2010, falling by 88%. While recent contributions have started to reverse this trend, the United States' contribution to humanitarian response in Somalia still stands at only 15% of the international total, compared against a US share of 40% to 50% in the rest of the region. The US is the largest global donor to humanitarian relief, and other donors often follow our lead. If the US steps up its assistance to the region, particularly to Somalia, this could have a powerful multiplier effect by influencing the behavior of other donors.

CHALLENGES TO THE RESPONSE

There are several important reasons why the impact of the drought is proving so much more severe in southern Somalia than elsewhere in the region. The first is the long history of insecurity in the south, which has impeded aid actors and prevented development investments. Even before the southern militias imposed restrictions on aid access, the history of insecurity in the area prevented the sort of sustained food security and development programming that has been common in Kenya and Ethiopia. These programs build resiliency, improve natural resource management, and help people to mitigate the challenges posed by cyclical droughts. Southern Somalia has not benefitted from this kind of aid, and has been left less resilient to drought than its neighbors.

The next factor, as has been widely reported, is the restrictions on aid access by southern militias, and accompanying security risks to aid groups. The challenges to aid groups in the south have been well-documented, including in the recent report by the UN's Monitoring Group for Somalia.[13] The report describes how aid groups were able to operate relatively freely in the south until 2010, when the operating environment deteriorated significantly as the militias began to impose unacceptable conditions on aid groups. Those conditions, which were inconsistent with core humanitarian principles, contributed to decisions by many aid groups to scale back their work. By the time that Mercy Corps and other aid groups were formally expelled from the south in September 2010, we had few operations left there in any case because of the deteriorating operating environment. It is important to note here that we and other groups have continued to operate in the northern and central regions of the country.

The final obstacle has been US legal restrictions on aid funding to Somalia, which predate the expulsion of aid groups by the militias. Reviewing the background of these restrictions is important not because I believe them to have been the principal obstacle to aiding southern Somalia – they were not. But these restrictions have been the only such obstacle that the US Government could unilaterally take out of the way. We are encouraged by the recent indications from the Administration that these restrictions have now been modified to allow greater support to relief efforts in the south. We have some remaining concerns about how the new arrangement will be implemented, particularly the fact that it only applies to programs that are wholly or partly funded by the US Government. This provides no protection to interventions implemented by US organization with funding from private foundations or European donors, for example. We hope to address those issues swiftly, but nonetheless the Administration should be commended for its willingness to alter the overall restrictions in light of the ongoing emergency. With this issue hopefully moving in a positive direction, I do not wish to dwell overly long on the past. But it is important, even as we look forward, to take stock of what we have until now been unable to do, and draw lessons from that.

The challenges that have arisen from the legal restrictions on aid to Somalia over the past several years are fundamentally systemic. Despite the best efforts of the professionals at USAID, the restrictions have several times caused serious delays in the efforts of USAID and US relief groups to provide aid to Somalia. USAID, for its part, has faced a thicket of legal and political obstacles but has consistently done its utmost to deal with those in a way that enables responsible aid to continue. Throughout our deliberations over the past several years, USAID's professionals have been collaborative and constructive. The blame for the delays and obstacles ultimately lies with the nature of the restrictions themselves. They are overly broad, allowing automatic humanitarian exemptions only for medical supplies and religious materials. Obtaining humanitarian exemptions for anything outside of those two categories typically requires a license that is only approved after a cumbersome and lengthy interagency process. This is a system that cries out for serious review, as I believe the last two years have demonstrated.

The restrictions first became an obstacle in Somalia in April 2009, when USAID raised concerns that some US resources might be diverted in violation of US Government prohibitions on material support to groups designated by the US as terrorists. It was reported at the time that USAID was seeking an OFAC license for its work in Somalia, but that the Treasury Department was reluctant to grant this. Over the summer of 2009, USAID stopped processing new humanitarian response grants to UN agencies and NGOs while deliberations over a path forward dragged on.[14] In the midst of a serious humanitarian crisis in much of the country, numerous US-funded humanitarian response programs were suspended as grant agreements expired and could not be renewed. An agreement was finally struck in late October of that year – nearly seven months after the issue first arose – to allow funding to move forward in FY2010.[15]

However, when the FY2010 grants began to expire in early FY2011, USAID again suspended grant processing. By this point, most UN and NGO partners were no longer operating in southern Somalia, and the grant requests that were held up were instead for northern and central regions of Somalia, which are not under the control of US-designated militant groups. By the time the FY2010 grants began expiring, the fall 2010 rainy season in Somalia had failed and it was clear that a dire humanitarian situation would arise in the coming months. Several months passed as the Administration sought a way out of the impasse. In late spring, UN and NGO partners entered into negotiations with USAID over whether to resume funding. An agreement to allow USAID to resume humanitarian funding to northern and central Somalia was finally struck in May of this year – nearly eight months into FY2011.

The eight months that were lost were a period in which the humanitarian community was well aware of the prospect of severe drought and famine. This was the very period when the US Government's UN and NGO partners could have been working full-tilt to prepare for the coming calamity. While the south was not accessible to us at that point, a great deal could have been done to preposition, prepare communities in accessible regions of the country, and assist the already-large flows of internally displaced people. Yet the bureaucratic tie-up over US legal restrictions left UN and NGO partners unable to obtain USG resources that would have enabled a much more robust response in the northern and central regions. This has been particularly damaging in central Somalia, which has been afflicted with drought every bit as severe as the southern areas, and also hosts tens of thousands of displaced southerners in desperate conditions.

THE ROAD AHEAD

The situation across the Horn of Africa is likely to worsen in the coming months as water sources dwindle and people's stocks of food and money are depleted. In southern Somalia – assuming that the Administration's moves to relax the legal restrictions will enable aid groups to resume programs there – many agencies will be eager to move ahead with relief efforts. The NGO community is strongly committed to ensuring that aid is not diverted away from those who need it most. I would emphasize that we do not know exactly what to expect in terms of access and security, and we do not discount the very real challenges that remain. But there are some reasons for cautious optimism, including the recent success of United Nations agencies and the International Committee of the Red Cross in making initial aid distributions freely and without interference. [16]

The recent report of the UN's Somalia Monitoring Group described how access for aid groups often varies considerably in different regions of the south, depending on local political and clan dynamics and their interplay with higher-level political factors. That dynamic will largely shape the opportunities for response in southern Somalia, and provides further grounds for cautious optimism over what may be achievable. Regardless of the high-level political movements – positive or negative – aid groups will ultimately have to negotiate terms of safe and effective access with local leaders in communities across the south. Many aid groups will choose to work with or support local Somali civil society organizations, which have capacity and long experience working on humanitarian response. This will result in a sort of "patchwork quilt" approach to assistance provision, with different agencies providing aid in whichever communities they are able to safely access. These arrangements are likely to remain highly fluid, and aid groups will have to show extreme flexibility and responsiveness to seize new opportunities quickly.

Beyond southern Somalia, there is a great deal that can be done to prevent the rest of the region from descending into famine conditions. The humanitarian community has learned a great deal over the past few decades about how to deal more effectively with food crises. No longer does the international response to famine and drought center mainly on camps and food distribution. Instead, we follow several "best practices" learned from past disasters:

- Work with markets, not against them: Mass food distribution is not always the best way to deal with a food crisis; it can sometimes distort and undermine local markets, put, merchants out of business, and degrade important market supply links. Mass hunger is not a result simply of inadequate local food production, but rather of inadequate resources amongst the population to access food through their normal means. This remains the case in the Horn, even in much of southern Somalia: food can be found in the markets, but it is priced well beyond the means of those who need it. This means that food voucher and cash-based interventions, which enable people to afford food, will be an important tool for combating hunger. These interventions can also be more efficient than distributing food aid, since they do not require the transport and importation of food nor complicated distribution networks. In-kind food aid will likely be needed to supplement what is available in markets, but should not be the automatic first resort.

- Preserve livelihoods, not just lives: Interventions that seek to support the livelihoods of at-risk populations, as well as save lives, will bear helpful dividends. The most effective way to mitigate long-term impacts of the drought is to provide assistance that protects the remnants of people's livelihoods in the near term and helps them to rebuild their livelihoods quickly in the medium term. This means interventions to protect remaining animal stocks, like veterinary services and water trucking; and agricultural support to ensure that farmers need not miss the next planting season due to depleted seed stocks. These sorts of livelihood-focused activities will reduce the need for prolonged humanitarian support. [17]

- Pay attention to health: In the 1991-92 famine in Somalia, the return of rain ironically posed major health challenges because the drought-weakened population was extra-vulnerable to water-borne diseases. Food aid and livelihoods support is not enough to save lives in this kind of situation – aggressive health care and emergency nutrition interventions are also necessary. Opportunistic diseases that prey on a weakened population will otherwise claim many lives.

- Help people where they are: Aid programs that assist people where they are, rather than inducing them to displace to other areas, are both more efficient and more humane than camp-based interventions. Preventing displacement minimizes social and economic disruptions, enables continuation of livelihood activities, and avoids the arduous and dangerous process of abrupt relocation. It also avoids creation of semi-permanent refugee and displacement camps, which are expensive to maintain and often hard to close down once a crisis ends.

- Invest in long-term resiliency: Even as we focus on the immediate crisis, the aid community and aid donors should be thinking hard about how to build better resiliency to this type of crisis. While this drought is extremely severe, lesser droughts have become a common occurrence in the Horn in recent years and are becoming a permanent fixture. Avoiding future humanitarian crises will require that we seek to work with governments and community leaders to help at-risk populations to better manage their natural resources and develop successful coping mechanisms. This must be a long-term investment and will need to be sustained by donors even after the energy around the current crisis has waned. Fortunately, sustaining longer-term investments in resiliency will save money over the long term by mitigating the impact of recurring droughts on the population, thus reducing the need for frequent humanitarian assistance.

We know what we must do; what remains in question is whether we will be able to do it. This rests on two important unknowns. The first is whether the region at large – Somalia, Kenya, Ethiopia, Djibouti – will receive sufficient resources to enable humanitarian agencies and regional governments to respond aggressively to mounting needs. The second is whether obstacles to humanitarian access in southern Somalia – principally the local restrictions and security threats, but also legal restrictions amongst donor states – will be removed in order to enable a response to scale up in that region. With these unknowns in mind, I would like to leave the committee with several recommendations:

1) Ensure a robust US Government response: As noted above, the US response this year stands at less than half of what the Bush Administration contributed to the region's drought response in 2008. While the US and global contributions this year are generous, they do not approach the level that will be required to avoid a large-scale catastrophe – as Secretary Clinton herself acknowledged on July 20th.[18] USAID did a good job of regional prepositioning, and has been rapidly churning out new grants over the past month as the full scope of the disaster has emerged. But real questions remain about whether the US will be able to step up like it did in 2008. The FY2012 outlook is not encouraging, with the House of Representative proposing to slash the very accounts that are financing the US government response: Food for Peace (a 30% proposed cut below FY11 levels,

and 50% below FY08 levels); International Disaster Assistance (a 12% proposed cut below FY11 levels); and Migration and Refugee Assistance (an 11% proposed cut below FY11 levels). Enacting such cuts in the face of the worst famine the world has seen in several decades would be disastrous, and I would urge the Senate to ensure that these accounts are protected in the FY2012 budget deliberations. But I suspect that even more must be done. In years past, a disaster of this magnitude would have been cause for a supplemental – like the three billion dollar supplemental that was passed last year to support the Haiti response. I would urge the Congress to consider a supplemental budget appropriation to address this crisis.

2) Engage the American public: Despite the severity of this crisis, there has been relatively little of the sort of active public engagement that we saw following the recent disasters in Haiti and Japan. This is troubling, because the ability of American aid organizations to respond robustly to a humanitarian disasters tends to track closely with the level of American popular engagement in the crisis. I would encourage all members of Congress, as they head back to their districts for the August recess, to alert their constituents to the severity of what is now taking place in the Horn of Africa. I would also urge the White House to be much more vocal about this crisis. As we saw after the Haiti earthquake, calls by the President and First Lady for generosity can have a tremendous galvanizing impact on the American public. The ideal scenario might involve joint appeals by Administration and Congressional leaders to demonstrate that responding to human suffering on such a massive scale transcends political boundaries.

3) Reform legal restrictions on US response: As I noted earlier, the legal restrictions imposed under the Patriot Act and related law have thrown up significant roadblocks to the humanitarian response and impeded preparedness. The safety valve provided by OFAC licensing is useful and we hope that the Administration's recent announcement will be implemented in a way that truly enables us to provide relief without fear of legal exposure. As a general rule of thumb, we would ask that the protections now extended to USAID through their OFAC license be extended in full to USAID's partners as well. But this development notwithstanding, we have seen over the past two years that obtaining an OFAC license if often politically difficult and massively time-consuming. The fact that OFAC restrictions harmed

US capacity to prepare for and respond to a famine that was anticipated months in advance should give Congress pause. I suspect that those who wrote the laws did not have this sort of outcome in mind. I would strongly advise that Congress re-examine the interplay between OFAC restrictions and humanitarian aid, and explore whether a more streamlined and responsive approach can be found. A good place to start would be by expanding the list of exempted categories beyond medical supplies and religious materials, to also include assistance related to food, water, and shelter needs.

I wish to sincerely thank the Sub-Committee for its focus on this tremendously important issue, and for extending me the privilege of testifying today.

End Notes

[1] FEWSNET/FSNAU: Evidence for a Famine Declaration (July 19, 2011)

[2] USAID FEWS-NET: East Africa: Past year one of the driest on record in the eastern Horn (June 14, 2011)

[3] USAID FEWS-NET: East Africa Food Security Outlook Update (July 2011)

[4] FSNAU, FEWS-NET: Somalia Dekadal Food Security and Nutrition Monitoring (July 25, 2011)

[5] Voice of America: African Refugee Children at High Risk for Kalaazar Malaria Viral Infections (July 27, 2011)

[6] FEWSNET/FSNAU: Evidence for a Famine Declaration (July 19, 2011)

[7] UNICEF ESARO, Horn of Africa Crisis: Situation Report #2 (July 28, 2011)

[8] UNOCHA: Humanitarian Requirements for the Horn of Africa Drought (July 28, 2011)

[9] USAID FEWS-NET: Kenya Enhanced Food Security Monitoring (July 22, 2011)

[10] USAID, WFP, FEWS-NET Special Report: Kenya Food Security (June 2011)

[11] UNOCHA: Humanitarian Requirements for the Horn of Africa Drought (July 28, 2011)

[12] UN OCHA Financial Tracking System: Somalia Emergencies for 2008 - Total Humanitarian Funding per Donor; UN OCHA Financial Tracking System: Somalia Emergencies for 2011 - Total Humanitarian Funding per Donor

[13] UN: Monitoring Group Report on Somalia and Eritrea (July 18, 2011)

[14] New York Times: U.S. Delays Somalia Aid, Fearing it is Feeding Terrorists (October 1, 2009)

[15] IRIN: US Government to Set New Aid Terms (October 6, 2009)

[16] Devex: Aid Reaches Famine-Hit Region in Southern Somalia (July 27, 2011)

[17] ALNAP: Slow-onset Disasters - Drought and Food and Livelihoods Insecurity (2007)

[18] Secretary Clinton: U.S. Response to Declaration of Famine in Somalia and Drought in the Horn of Africa (July 20, 2011)

In: Humanitarian Crisis and Response ...   ISBN: 978-1-61942-540-8
Editors: C.J. Newsome and H.I. Herron © 2012 Nova Science Publishers, Inc.

Chapter 6

DROUGHT & FAMINE HEARING–
PHAM TESTIMONY

J. Peter Pham

Mr. Chairman, Ranking Member Isakson, Distinguished Members of the Subcommittee:

I would like to thank you very much for the opportunity to testify today on the drought and famine conditions in the Horn of Africa in general and in Somalia in particular, as well as on the response of the United States and other members of the international community to this growing crisis.

As we meet, the situation especially critical—the head of the United Nations refugee agency describes it as the "worst humanitarian disaster" in the world today—with nearly half of the Somali population, some 3.7 million people, facing starvation while at least another 11 million men, women, and children across the Horn of Africa are thought to be at risk.

Given this grim reality, the first concern of the international community is, understandably, focused where it should be anyway: getting relief to the victims. However, in addressing immediate needs, attention should also be paid to the broader geopolitical context as well as the long-term implications of the challenges before us. Since other witnesses testifying today are better to positioned, individually and institutionally, to address the technical questions relating to the scope of the crisis, its impact on vulnerable populations, and the logistics of getting assistance to them, I will concentrate on four key points which I believe the United States and other responsible international actors should bear in mind in assessing the current situation and determining adequate responses to it, as well as planning longer-term engagement with this region:

1. *Al-Shabaab's responsibility in exacerbating the crisis.* While the group cannot be blamed for the desertification trends, climate change, and meteorological conditions, the violent conflict it has engaged in and the economic and political policies it has pursued have certainly worsened a bad situation.
2. *Far from being a part of the solution, Somalia's "Transitional Federal Government" (TFG) is part of the problem—in fact, a not insignificant cause of the ongoing crisis.* The regime's unelected officials may be preferable to the insurgents seeking to overthrow them, but they represent, at best, the international community's choice for the lesser of two evils.
3. *The sheer number of people on the move in and from Somali territory will have enormous and possibly permanent consequences for the region.* The potential population shifts threaten to upend delicate political balances as well as present new security challenges for the Horn of Africa and beyond.
4. *Amid the crisis, there is, nonetheless, an opportunity to promote stability and security within Somalia, if not across the Horn of Africa.* In fact, there is a narrow window of opportunity during which it might be possible to seriously weaken and possibly even finish al-Shabaab as a major force in Somali politics once and for all.

AL-SHABAAB'S ROLE IN THE CRISIS

Harakat al-Shabaab al-Mujahideen ("Movement of Warrior Youth," al-Shabaab) is not only linked ideologically with the global jihadist ideology of al-Qaeda and, increasingly, operationally with Yemen-based al-Qaeda in the Arabian Peninsula (AQAP), it is also an entity that richly deserves to opprobrium for its singular role in making what in any event would have been a very bad situation far, far worse.

There is no doubt that the insecurity it has caused since it began its violent insurgency four years ago added greatly to the sufferings of the Somali people. Moreover, while al-Shabaab is far from a monolithic organization, its leadership does have a history of denying access to the areas under its control to UN relief agencies like UNICEF and the World Food. For their part, as is now well known, last year the international agencies as well as several nongovernmental organizations pulled out of several areas under the control of al-Shabaab after several aid workers were killed and the group began imposing strict conditions on their remaining colleagues, extorting "security fees" and "taxes." Moreover, because al-Shabaab has been designated as an international terrorist organization by the United States and a number of other countries, NGOs have avoided working in areas it controls for fear of running afoul of laws against providing material support to terrorist groups.

As a matter of fact—one which a number of analysts, including myself, have noted for some time and which was confirmed by the annual report to the UN Security Council by its Sanctions Monitoring Group for Somalia and Eritrea, a document released just last week—although alShabaab has profited, either by diversion or "taxation," from humanitarian aid, the amounts represented at most a small fraction of its overall revenue stream. Consequently, it heartening to see that the administration is working to clarify and, where necessary, ease the relevant restrictions in order to facilitate the work of humanitarian organizations.

A far more important source of income for the group is, in fact, more directly related to the humanitarian crisis: the industrial production for export of charcoal. While people living between the Juba and Shabelle rivers in southern Somalia have gathered charcoal for their own use from the region's acacia forests from time immemorial, it is only in the last few years that the production has reached its present unsustainable levels. It is estimated that somewhere around two-thirds of the forests which used to cover some 15 percent of Somali territory has been reduced to chunks of "black gold," packed into 25-kilogram bags, and shipped to countries in the Persian Gulf which have themselves banned the domestic production of charcoal. The UN Monitoring Group conservatively estimates that up to 4.5 million of these sacks are exported each year, primarily through the port of Kismayo, which has been controlled by al-Shabaab or other forces allied to its cause since September 2008, earning the group millions of dollars in profits. Meanwhile, where once there were the old-growth acacia stands, thorn bushes now proliferate, rendering the areas useless to the Somali people, whether they be pastoralists or agriculturalists (the former graze their livestock in the grass that flourishes where the root systems of acacia groves hold in ground water and prevent erosion, while the latter grow staple crops in neighboring lands so long as there are tree stands holding in top soil), and contributing further to the desertification that is always a persistent threat in a land as arid or semi-arid as

Somalia. Thus, it was both simultaneously tragic and ironic that, when a heavy rain came briefly this past weekend to what was formerly the country's breadbasket, the result was not deliverance, but disaster as, absent any foliage to help absorb the precipitation, flash floods compounded the misery in several places.

Al-Shabaab also operates a complex system of taxation on residents within areas it controls and imposes levies not just on aid groups, but also businesses, sales transactions, and land. The tax on arable land in particular has had the effect of changing the political economy of farming communities which previously eked out a living just above subsistence. For example, in Bakool and Lower Shabelle—precisely the two areas at the epicenter of the famine—communities used to grow their own food and, whenever possible, stored any surplus sorghum or maize against times of hardship. However, when al-Shabaab imposed a monetary levy on acreage, farmers were pushed into growing cash crops like sesame which could be sold to traders connected with the Islamist movement's leadership for export in order to obtain the funds to pay the obligatory "jihad war contributions." However rich in anti-oxidants sesame seeds may be, they are of rather limited value for purposes of food security.

If all this were not bad enough, once the famine set in, al-Shabaab leaders have alternated between denying the crisis—arguing instead that accounts of hunger were being "exaggerated" in order to undermine their hold over the populace—and preventing affected people from moving in search of food. Whether or not it is a formal policy of the group or not, there are credible reports from sources on the ground of at least several "holding areas" in Lower Shabelle where al-Shabaab forces are using force or the threat thereof to prevent displaced people from leaving its territory to find help.

SOMALIA'S DYSFUNCTIONAL TFG

In Congressional testimony two years ago, I noted that the TFG was "not a government by any common-sense definition of the term: it is entirely dependent on foreign troops...to protect its small enclave in Mogadishu, but otherwise administers no territory; even within this restricted zone, it has shown no functional capacity to govern, much less provide even minimal services to its citizens." And that was *before* the famine.

Despite the fact that, at not inconsiderable sacrifice, the African Union Mission in Somalia (AMISOM) peacekeeping force protecting the regime has managed to extend its operational reach to now be present in thirteen of Mogadishu's sixteen districts—although the force commander, Ugandan Major General Nathan Mugisha, acknowledges that his troops "dominate" in just "more than half of these"—the TFG remains hobbled by corruption and infighting. Quite frankly, the so-called "government" lead by Sheikh Sharif Sheikh Ahmed is little better than a criminal enterprise—one that its own auditors reported stole more than 96 percent of the bilateral assistance it received in the years 2009 and 2010. The findings contained in the UN Monitoring Group report were perhaps even more damning: "Diversion of arms and ammunition from the Transitional Federal Government and its affiliated militias has been another significant source of supply to arms dealers in Mogadishu, and by extension to alShabaab." The investigators even highlighted case where an RPG launcher and associated munitions, purchased for the regime under a U.S. State Department contract, found their way into a stronghold of al-Shabaab that AMISOM captured earlier this year.

It should thus come as no surprise that such "leaders" are of limited helpfulness in the face of the present humanitarian emergency. They are likely to see it as yet another opportunity to capture rents, especially since their already extended mandate expires in two weeks and it is for want of a ready-made "Plan B" that the international community is not taking issue with the TFG's leaders arbitrarily proroguing their terms of office by another year—although on what legal grounds is anyone's guess. (No wonder the official position of the Government of the United States, expressed in a brief filed before the U.S. Supreme Court last year by thenSolicitor-General Elena Kagan as well as the Legal Advisor of the Department of State, is that since the fall of the dictator Muhammad Siyad Barre in 1991, "the United States has not recognized any entity as the government of Somalia" and that federal courts should "not attach significance to statements of the TFG" absent specific guidance from the executive branch.)

MASS MIGRATION

Given this context, it should come as no surprise that Somalis are on the move. The Dabaab refugee camp in northeastern Kenya, which was built in 1992 during the last great Somali famine to temporarily house 90,000 people, nowadays hosts more than 400,000, with more than one thousand additional persons arriving each day. Another 112,000 refugees have found shelter in the Dollo Ado area of Ethiopia. And these are the lucky ones: it is estimated that there are possibly 1.5 million Somalis internally displaced within their own country, with some unfortunates even literally caught in the no man's land at outskirts of Mogadishu between the frontline positions of the insurgents and AMISOM troops. And, it needs to be emphasized that all of this is before the coming months when conditions are expected to be even worse.

Given the parlous conditions prevalent across the territory of the former Somali state (outside of Somaliland in the northwest, Puntland in the northeast, and possibly a few other places), it is virtually assured that any Somali who crosses the border into Kenya or Ethiopia is likely to become *ipso facto* a permanent emigrant (after all, Somalia's contemporary economy, it should not be forgotten, has been transformed into one built upon remittances from the Diaspora). In any event, since there has been no rush of third countries offering resettlement to the preexistent Somali refugee population before the famine, there is no reason to think that things will be different with the influx of new arrivals. Kenya and Ethiopia, however, are beset with complicated issues with their own ethnic Somali minorities; neither country is in much of a position to absorb hundreds of thousands, if not millions, of itinerant Somalis.

Consequently a population shift such as what we are witnessing in the Horn of Africa—a literal exodus of Biblical proportions--threatens to upend delicate political balances as well as present a host of new security challenges. In fact, concerns over security and the adequate screening (or lack thereof) of Somalis entering their country have already exposed one rift within Kenya's national unity government between Prime Minister Raila Odinga, who opened the border as a humanitarian gesture, and some of his ministers who oppose the move. A quick perusal of Kenyan newspapers is enough to confirm that this question will undoubtedly enjoy a high profile as the East African country enters its electoral season next year.

Thus, if they are not to cause, however unintentionally, even greater harm, responses to the mass migration set in motion first by the prolonged Somali crisis and now the famine need to take factor in these realities.

A CHANCE FOR STABILITY AND SECURITY

If one dares contemplate a silver lining to the current crisis—although it comes at a terrible price—it is that it has apparently caught al-Shabaab off guard.

For a long time, despite the extremist ideology espoused by its foreign-influenced leaders which set them outside the mainstream of Somali culture and society, al-Shabaab at could present itself as being better (even if harsher) rulers than the corrupt denizens of the TFG. The brutal *hudud* punishments its tribunals meted out, for example, may have been utterly alien from the Somali experience, but it was a rough justice nonetheless and better than the chaos and lawlessness that was the experience of many Somalis in the 1990s. Moreover, the group managed to wrap itself up in the mantle of Somali nationalism by portraying the African Union peacekeepers as foreign occupiers, although the fact that AMISOM troops are propping up the despised TFG and, in the process, cause civilian casualties, made this narrative all the more credible.

Within the last year, however, AMISOM has improved its capabilities and managed to lower civilian casualties even as it pushed al-Shabaab forces back within Mogadishu. In addition, the famine and al-Shabaab's clumsy response to it have thoroughly dispelled any delusions about the "good governance" capabilities by the movement. Now the effects of famine are not only exacerbated by al-Shabaab, but the disaster has exposed divisions within the movement with some of its local councils and militias expressing a willingness to accept help even as the leadership continues to spurn it. Moreover, actions like the blocking of people trying to escape the famine will sap al-Shabaab of what remains of its popular legitimacy. (Of course, if one is seeking to use this opportunity to undermine al-Shabaab, it would be helpful if a prospect more attractive than domination by the venal TFG was offered to communities just freed from the militants' yoke.)

While there is undoubtedly some risk in sending aid areas where al-Shabaab operates, it is more probable that whatever negative effects the assistance will have will fall largely on the group, either as some of its local leaders defect or populations are weaned from their reliance on them. And there are organizations—not all of them necessarily international—with a track record of delivering assistance, even within al-Shabaab held areas, without allowing resources to be diverted. One that comes to mind is SAACID, the extraordinary nongovernmental organization founded and directed by Somali women, which is engaged in conflict transformation, women's empowerment, education, healthcare, emergency relief, employment schemes, and development. SAACID's *modus operandi* is a model for others. SAACID gets food from, among other partners, the World Food Program—when, that is, the latter agency has any. By working closely with clan elders and community members, it embeds itself in its immediate surroundings and thus can carry on in areas where, for example, the WFP can no longer go because the presence of al-Shabaab. Thus, during the height of the fighting in Mogadishu in recent years, SAACID was literally the only entity that was present in all sixteen of the capital's districts, providing some 80,000 2,000-calorie meals daily to some of the most vulnerable residents.

Such a model is one way the international community can get assistance to drought-affected populations and do so where they are, rather than requiring that these poor people displace themselves and, consequently, create additional challenges which will have to be dealt with further down the road after the initial emergency has passed.

And it goes without saying that should security be improved in Somalia and the mass emigration halted, if not reversed, the prospects for the increasingly important subregion at the crossroads of the Africa and the Middle East will brighten immensely.

CONCLUSION

Confronted with the dreadful specter of mass starvation on a scale not seen in more than half a century, the priority most assuredly is to get life-giving assistance to those most at risk and to do so in the most timely, efficient, and effective manner possible. However, urgency is no dispensation from the ethical and political responsibility both to understand to what caused or heightened the emergency and to consider the possible consequences of any proposed responses to it. Increased material resources are clearly needed, but even more, what is required is sustained engagement and not a little bit of strategic vision.

In: Humanitarian Crisis and Response ...   ISBN: 978-1-61942-540-8
Editors: C.J. Newsome and H.I. Herron © 2012 Nova Science Publishers, Inc.

Chapter 7

AL SHABAAB AND THE CHALLENGES OF PROVIDING HUMANITARIAN ASSISTANCE IN SOMALIA

Katherine L. Zimmerman

Somalia is one of the most inimical countries to humanitarian aid workers. The security context and the humanitarian operational environment that both local and international aid agencies face have severely restricted humanitarian activities, particularly in areas under the control of the radical Islamist group, al Shabaab. Aid organizations responded to al Shabaab's threats by limiting areas of operations or fully suspending operations in southern Somalia. The majority of the organizations that remain active in Somalia have concentrated operations in and around territory under government control in Mogadishu, territory under the control of government-aligned administrations in central Somalia, and in the semiautonomous regions in northern Somalia of Puntland and Somaliland. In the south, the withdrawal of humanitarian aid organizations has exacerbated the effect of the Horn's severe drought on the Somali people.

The drought in the Horn of Africa has left over 3.2 million Somalis in need of immediate food assistance. Of these, 2.8 million live in southern Somalia, an area that has proven to be the most inaccessible in the country. There is a famine in Bay and Lower Shabelle region, in parts of Middle Shabelle and Bakool regions, in the internally displaced persons (IDP) camps in the Afgoi Corridor, and also in the IDP camps in Mogadishu. The UN has noted that two other regions, Lower and Middle Jubba regions, are expected to be experiencing famine conditions. The hardest-hit regions remain under the control of al Shabaab.

Denial of access by al Shabaab militants, and in some cases by other armed militias, is the single greatest obstacle to the provision of humanitarian assistance, as noted in the UN's most recent monitoring group report. Al Shabaab not only creates a prohibitive security environment, but also restricts humanitarian operations in southern Somalia. The group has banned many international aid agencies from operating within territories under its control. Al Shabaab has enforced this ban with violence: militants raid local offices, destroy foodstuffs and medical supplies, and kidnap aid workers. The group's actions against aid organizations have created the humanitarian emergency that many Somalis now face.

AL SHABAAB'S HISTORY WITH HUMANITARIAN ASSISTANCE

Al Shabaab has increasingly become an obstacle to the delivery of humanitarian assistance in Somalia, the majority of which consists of food aid. There has been an evolution in al Shabaab's position toward international aid organizations. Over the years, the group has solidified its stance against the activities of aid organizations, claiming that many American and UN-funded organizations have a "Christian" agenda and do not pursue the best interests of the Somali people. Local non-governmental organizations (NGOs) have also faced pressure from al Shabaab to end their activities. The group has frequently accused aid workers of spying for Western intelligence agencies or has targeted those organizations whose operations also support residents living under the authority of the UN-backed Transitional Federal Government (TFG).

On July 20, 2009, al Shabaab announced its establishment of the Office for the Supervision of the Affairs of Foreign Agencies (OSAFA) to monitor the movements of all NGOs and international organizations operating within Somalia. The same day, al Shabaab accused the United Nations Development Program (UNDP), the United Nations Department of Security and Safety (UNDSS), and the United Nations Political Office for Somalia (UNPOS) of engaging in activities deemed hostile to Islam and ordered all of the organizations' offices closed. Al Shabaab militants immediately enforced this edict, raiding the UN offices in Baidoa in Bay region and in Wajid in Bakool region. The group had already forced CARE and the International Medical

Corps to close on suspicion that the two organizations provided the intelligence leading to the successful U.S. airstrike on former al Shabaab leader Aden Hashi Ayro. By November 2009, the local al Shabaab administration in Bay and Bakool regions required that humanitarian aid agencies abide by 11 conditions, including a registration fee, the removal of all logos from vehicles, and a ban on female employees.

Al Shabaab leadership particularly targeted the UN's World Food Program (WFP), severely impacting its operations in southern Somalia. In early November 2009, al Shabaab deputy leader Sheikh Mukhtar Robow Ali, also known as Abu Mansur, accused the WFP of destroying Somalia's local agriculture market through its distributions of food aid during harvest time and banned branded aid, including aid with the American flag on it. Al Shabaab then ordered the WFP to only purchase food from local farmers and to clear out all food warehouses by the end of the year. On January 1, 2010, al Shabaab militants raided a WFP warehouse in Marka, a coastal city in Lower Shabelle region, and burned over 300 sacks of food, claiming that the food had expired. The WFP responded by suspending its operations in Wajid, Bu'aale, Garbaharey, Afmadow, Jilib, and Beledweyne, citing a lack of security. The WFP has not been able to resume operations in southern Somalia.

The experience of the WFP was not unique; over the course of 2010, al Shabaab's shura council consolidated power and enforced bans on humanitarian aid agencies. By mid-September, at least seven other agencies were banned from Somalia, including Mercy Corps, Med-Aid, Horn Relief, World Vision, ADRA, Diakonia, and Famine Early Warning Systems Network (FEWS NET). Al Shabaab was able to enforce this ban in Kismayo, Lower and Middle Shabelle regions, Hiraan region, and Lower and Middle Jubba regions. For those organizations that remained operational, access to communities became more restricted as the power structure of al Shabaab became more centralized in the shura council. These organizations also faced restrictions on their activities and were subjected to taxation. The conditions that forced the suspension of humanitarian aid activity in areas under al Shabaab's control continued into 2011 and remain in force today.

CURRENT CONDITIONS UNDER AL SHABAAB

People who have fled al Shabaab-controlled territory in southern Somalia tell the same story – that draconian measures imposed upon the local population have driven many to leave. Local al Shabaab administrations follow the group's strict interpretation of *shari'a*, enforcing public observance of its laws with corporal punishments. Al Shabaab requires that both men and women abide by what it has determined to be Islamic dress and that women work only in the home and receive a male relative escort when out in public. The group has banned such activities as listening to music or watching soccer. There are reports that school-aged children have been forced to attend sessions with al Shabaab officials, to receive either religious or military training. In some cases, al Shabaab has required that every family provide a son to fight for the group, or pay $50 per month. In addition to forced conscription, al Shabaab exacts taxes from local communities and businessmen. Further, local aid workers have noted that al Shabaab has repeatedly threatened them.

Many of the communities living under al Shabaab have been in need of food aid for months and the drought that has affected the region has compounded this need. Local community elders called on al Shabaab to lift its restriction on humanitarian assistance in April 2011 and warned of imminent starvation should food aid not arrive. Certain humanitarian aid organizations do have access to al Shabaab-controlled territories, such as Islamic Relief and the International Committee of the Red Cross (ICRC); however, these organizations remain limited in their capabilities to combat the spread of famine.

On July 6, al Shabaab spokesman Sheikh Ali Mohamed Rage announced, "All aid agencies whose objective is only humanitarian relief are free to operate" in al Shabaab-controlled territory and required that these agencies contact al Shabaab's "Drought Committee." Rage later clarified that the ban on certain agencies, such as the WFP, remained in effect and denied that there was a famine in Somalia. There are reports that local al Shabaab administrations may be more amenable than al Shabaab's shura council to cooperation with larger international aid organizations. UNICEF, for example, landed a plane of food and medical supplies in al Shabaab-controlled Baidoa, the capital of Bay region. By and large, however, al Shabaab has remained hostile to many humanitarian aid agencies, claiming that they hold political agendas. Rage said of the famine, "Yes, there is drought, but the conditions are not as bad as they say. [The aid agencies] have another objective and it wouldn't surprise us if they were politicizing the situation." Al Shabaab's leader, Sheikh Mukhtar Abu Zubair, reiterated this sentiment, "Aid agencies and some countries declared famine and pretend they want to help you. They do so for these reasons: for trade purposes, to convert you from your religion and to colonize you."

Al Shabaab administrations have exploited local food resources, to the detriment of communities. As the conditions have deteriorated, al Shabaab has made exacting demands on the population. For example, in Bu'aale district in Middle Shabelle region, al Shabaab demanded a payment of $30 for every hectare of arable land along Jubba River. In Afmadow in Lower Jubba region, some residents were required to feed al Shabaab militants, facing punishment should they refuse to do so. In Afgoi outside of Mogadishu, reports say that al Shabaab executed local herders who had refused to turn over animals for slaughter to the group. Al Shabaab militants have also diverted river water to commercial farmers who provide financial support for the group. Widespread relief efforts in these regions remain impossible because of al Shabaab. Those relief efforts that are conducted remain smaller in scale and many are run under the auspices of al Shabaab administrations.

The severity of the situation in southern Somalia has driven many families to seek humanitarian assistance in areas outside of al Shabaab's control. An estimated 1,500 people arrive daily in Kenya's Dadaab refugee camp, and about two to three hundred refugees arrive in Ethiopia's Dolo Ado camp. The journey to the camp carries risks – banditry and armed militias throughout Somalia pose a threat to displaced persons. In some cases, al Shabaab has taken action to prevent Somalis from leaving its territory. The group has established roadblocks along primary routes used by refugees and has forced truckloads of people to return from where they came. For example, al Shabaab established roadblocks and checkpoints along the roads near Dhobley, a town on the Kenyan border, preventing many from gaining access to assistance across the border. Militants have also frequently inhibited Somalis' entry into TFG-controlled territory in Mogadishu. Overall, al Shabaab has consistently denied freedom of movement to Somalis living under its control.

PROSPECTS FOR HUMANITARIAN ASSISTANCE IN SOUTHERN SOMALIA

It is necessary to recognize very real restrictions on humanitarian aid activities when considering the prospects of expanding operations into southern Somalia.

The humanitarian operating environment is precarious in the country even without the presence of al Shabaab. There have been few improvements on the security conditions since the UN first deployed a peacekeeping force in 1992 to secure the supply lines for humanitarian aid delivery. The only clear realized gains have been made in Mogadishu, where a peacekeeping force assists the weak, UN-backed TFG. The African Union Mission in Somalia (AMISOM) has a force presence of about 9,000 Ugandan and Burundian peacekeepers. Territory outside of the TFG and AMISOM's security perimeter has often been contested by various armed factions, and it is likely that any insertion of resources into such an environment will result in violence as it did in the early 1990s. There have already been documented attacks on aid convoys in Bay and Hiraan regions, during which at least one aid worker was killed. A significant escalation in humanitarian activities throughout southern Somalia will very likely increase the risks to aid workers' safety.

Though al Shabaab is not the sole guarantor of security in Somalia, the group poses the greatest threat to aid workers in southern Somalia. Al Shabaab's shura council has made clear that it will not accept the presence of international humanitarian aid organizations and that it will enforce this ban with violence. This fact remains true even as humanitarian conditions continue to deteriorate in areas under al Shabaab's control. Humanitarian aid organizations are ill-equipped to deal with the threat posed to their personnel by al Shabaab militants and it would be naïve to ignore the security aspect of any humanitarian operation in southern Somalia.

The international community should be under no illusions about the requirements of undertaking a humanitarian operation in southern Somalia. There is a high likelihood that any such operation, which would entail establishing security in the heartland of al Shabaab's territory, would be met with significant armed resistance. Al Shabaab's militias have already exhibited the ability to withstand AMISOM operations in Mogadishu, especially during its 2010 Ramadan offensive. During this offensive, al Shabaab militants successfully advanced the frontline of fighting toward AMISOM and TFG headquarters, despite the presence of 6,300 peacekeepers. It has taken a fifty percent increase in peacekeeping troops in Mogadishu and a sustained effort by the TFG to develop its own security forces to re-establish temporary control over the majority of the capital. Whereas in Mogadishu, al Shabaab conducted an insurgency against AMISOM and TFG troops, in southern Somalia, al Shabaab is the dominant power.

Al Shabaab has a very strong power base in major southern cities such as the ports of Marka and Kismayo. Al Shabaab is able to operate military training camps openly and will be able to call up forces quickly if challenged. An armed conflict in southern Somalia will likely require the deployment of Western ground forces, forces that could readily defeat al Shabaab militarily if called upon. The international community should not cling to the false belief that a humanitarian operation in southern Somalia could be successfully accomplished without ground forces supporting the mission.

The decision to pursue a humanitarian operation in southern Somalia ought to be made with these substantial costs in mind. Opting for a humanitarian aid operation in southern Somalia will require a military commitment. Seeking to purchase consent from or to cooperate with al Shabaab in order to insert humanitarian assistance into the south incurs future costs. Purchasing consent from al Shabaab does not guarantee future security or even the delivery of assistance to the people in need. What it does, however, is fund a virulent radical insurgent group that has stated its intentions to attack America and has increasingly established ties to al Qaeda's most operational franchise, al Qaeda in the Arabian Peninsula, across the Gulf of Aden in Yemen. Cooperating with al Shabaab will likely permit the group to dictate aid distribution, strengthening al Shabaab in its territories. A humanitarian operation to respond to the spreading famine, however morally imperative, must not be undertaken without a full understanding of the full requirements and the associated risks.

APPENDIX: MAP OF SOMALIA

In: Humanitarian Crisis and Response ...   ISBN: 978-1-61942-540-8
Editors: C.J. Newsome and H.I. Herron © 2012 Nova Science Publishers, Inc.

Chapter 8

EAST AFRICAN EMERGENCIES HEARING– SCRIBNER TESTIMONY

Shannon Scribner

Mr. Chairman, Congressman Payne, and Members of the Committee, thank you for the opportunity to testify today on the humanitarian situation in East Africa and the importance of a coordinated and sustainable US strategy. Oxfam is grateful for the work this committee has done to address the humanitarian situation affecting 12 million people today living in Ethiopia, Kenya and Somalia. We are also grateful for the leadership role the US government has played as the most generous donor, providing $600 million since the beginning of the year. Oxfam America is an international development and relief agency committed to developing lasting solutions to poverty, hunger and social injustice. We are part of a confederation of 15 Oxfam organizations working together in more than 100 countries with over 3,000 local partners around the globe.

In my testimony today, I will be outlining the humanitarian crisis in the region and providing recommendations for the US government's response based on the situation on the ground.

Oxfam's Response to the East Africa Crisis

Oxfam teams and partners are rapidly scaling up activities to provide lifesaving assistance in Ethiopia, Kenya, and Somalia through water and sanitation and food security and livelihoods interventions. Working with our partners, Oxfam is rehabilitating wells and boreholes, building latrines, providing sanitation and hygiene services, providing cash transfers and cash-for-work assistance and supporting livelihoods through activities such as rehabilitating livestock. We are currently reaching over 1 million people and aim to reach 3.5 million with emergency relief, while at the same time addressing long-standing threats to livelihoods and further building the resilience of the communities.

- In Somalia: Oxfam has worked with Somali partners for over 40 years with programs that focus on building the capacity of local nongovernmental organizations (NGOs) and Somali civil society to carry out both development and humanitarian activities. Through this network, Oxfam is able to support our partners in reaching hundreds of thousands of people in need throughout the country. Our partners have scaled up programs and seek to assist around 1.5 million people in 21 of south central Somalia's 45 districts. Our partners' programs include the single largest nutrition program in south central Somalia, which treats more than 12,000 severely malnourished children and pregnant and lactating mothers per month. We are also supporting the single largest public health program in Somalia, providing water and sanitation services to more than 250,000 displaced people in the Afgooye corridor and cash relief to over 16,000 vulnerable people.
- In Kenya, Oxfam's work combines development, campaigns and humanitarian response to contribute to the rights of communities in the Arid and Semi Arid Lands (ASALs) and in urban informal settlements. We also provide water and sanitation services in the Somali refugee camps of Dadaab in Kenya. In response to the current crisis we have scaled up our programs and aim to assist around 1 million people in Kenya. A key component of our work is providing cash to people affected by the drought so that they can buy food available in local markets. Our teams are drilling boreholes, rehabilitating water points and pumps, servicing generators that pump water from wells to communities and, where necessary, trucking water in and doing public health promotion work both for local

communities in Turkana and Wajir and in the refugee camps of Dadaab.

- In Ethiopia, Oxfam has been working with local NGOs and Ethiopian civil society since 1962, building the capacity of local organizations in the effective planning and management of both development and humanitarian programs. In the current crisis, Oxfam seeks to reach over 1 million people with water and sanitation services, health care, and cash relief to buy food. Our teams are providing income and livelihoods support through cash for work programs and livestock feeding and vaccinations, so that people can protect their most important productive asset – their animals. As several hundred Somali refugees cross the border into Dolo Ado every day, Oxfam is working to provide water and sanitation facilities for an estimated 20,000 people in Hiloweyn camp, one of five refugee camps in Liben zone in the southern part of Ethiopia's Somali region.

OVERVIEW

The Horn of Africa is experiencing its worst food crisis in years. The UN has declared that six areas of southern Somalia are experiencing famine conditions and it is currently estimated that half a million people are at the risk of death if they don't receive urgent assistance. All signs point to the crisis extending into 2012, and the after-effects of this crisis will be felt for years to come.

The famine and ongoing conflict in Somalia has resulted in large-scale population movements, internally and throughout the region. Thousands have fled from rural parts of Somalia into Mogadishu, while even more have walked for weeks or months to Kenya or Ethiopia in search of relief. In Kenya, 70 to 80 per cent of new arrivals are women and children and half of the children arriving are severely malnourished. According to the United Nations, there are 430,000 refugees living in Kenya's camps of Dadaab, making it the largest refugee camp in the world.

In Kenya, the number of people facing food insecurity is estimated at 3.75 million. There has been near total crop failure in marginal agricultural areas and national corn output for the season is expected to be 15 per cent below average. Food prices in local markets reached record levels in July, with the highest price increases in pastoral markets.

In Ethiopia, over 4.5 million people require emergency assistance, alongside over 250,000 refugees, mainly from Somalia. Ethiopia's Somali region and southern Oromia are among the worst-affected areas. In these regions, pastoralists have lost much of their livestock and it is anticipated that many more animals that families need to survive will die due to high disease prevalence among severely weakened livestock. In the Southern Nations, Nationalities, and Peoples region, corn and sorghum crops have failed in many areas, and since January, the price of corn has increased by 150-200%.

In Somalia, ongoing conflict, poverty, insecurity and recurrent natural disasters have led to a severe humanitarian crisis. This week, the United Nations declared the country's Bay region to be experiencing famine, bringing the total number of famine areas up to six. Bay has been classified as having Global Acute Malnutrition rates of 58% and Severe Acute Malnutrition rates of 22%. Both figures massively exceed the respective emergency thresholds of 15% and 2%. The total number of people now living in famine conditions in Somalia is 750,000. There is an expectation that the famine could expand to parts of Gedo, Juba, Middle Shabelle and Hiraan regions in the coming weeks.

It is no coincidence that the epicenter of the crisis is also the place where it is most difficult to provide humanitarian assistance to those most in need. Ongoing conflict and insecurity, insufficient provision of social services for the population, limited freedom for local organizations and the politicization of aid both by parties to the conflict and donor governments have all played a part in preventing Somalis from receiving the help they need and deserve. Despite these challenges, our experience has shown that aid can be delivered and people can be reached if those delivering the aid are accepted by the local communities and if the aid is not linked to political or military agendas. Through Somali partners, we are currently reaching 800,000 people in Somalia and aim to reach 1.5 million as part of our emergency response.

The scale and severity of this crisis is unparalleled. The situation is set to worsen and swift action is needed to save lives and avoid further suffering. The severe drought, with some of the driest conditions we have seen in 60 years, triggered this disaster, but it is not the sole cause. The conflict in Somalia, entrenched poverty and decades of under-investment in small-scale food producers have also contributed significantly to the crisis, with pastoralists particularly hard hit.

According to the Food and Agriculture Organization of the United Nations (FAO), below- average precipitation is predicted for the November to January rains in south and central Somalia and the greater Mandera triangle where Kenya, Ethiopia and Somalia meet. This means that emergency conditions could persist well into March/April 2012. In southern Somalia, recovery may not start until the next harvest in August 2012.

FAILING TO RESPOND ADEQUATELY TO THE EARLY WARNING SIGNS

According to the Famine Early Warning Systems Network (FEWSNET), which is largely supported by USAID, back in August 2010, there were clear indications of the impending drought and its possible impacts on food security in the region. Initial warnings of increased risk were published even further back in April 2010, when the La Niña phenomenon was foreseen. While a massive humanitarian operation is now underway, little was done until the May 2011 rains failed – as was predicted by early warning systems.

Drought is common in many parts of Africa, but with early warning systems working, there is no real excuse for continued late responses to impending food emergencies. Looking forward, national governments, regional actors and the international community, including NGOs, must do a better job of coordinating a holistic response early on if food emergencies are to be avoided in the future. Recent droughts reveal a series of slow or delayed responses, including last year in the Sahel and Kenya during the 2008/9 drought. Such delays suggest a failure on the part of the national and international actors involved at multiple steps in the response. More should have been done to respond to these warnings, including strengthening the resilience of local communities to better endure drought and other shocks in the first place.

IMPROVING ACCESS TO FOOD

A number of factors have resulted in significantly reduced food production in the region this year, including the failed rains and harvests, conflict, weak infrastructure, restricted access to agricultural inputs, a lack of market integration and restrictions on movement and trade. Addressing these constraints to agricultural productivity will require long-term assistance to help food producers, many of whom are women, grow more food while preserving and even enhancing a diminishing natural resource base.

At the same time, it is important to provide immediate assistance that will increase people's access to food. With high and rising food prices, basic staples are simply not affordable for tens of thousands of people throughout the region. The majority of people in the worst affected areas have no savings and few safety nets to support them when drought or other disasters strike. Oxfam's assessments have shown that cash-based interventions are a rapid, effective way of saving lives, supporting livelihoods and contributing to local market functioning. As the World Food Program faces ongoing challenges in procuring enough food to meet the immense needs, we must work to ensure that food aid is available in areas where markets are not functioning and cash assistance is available in areas where markets are functioning and food is available.

Mass Displacement

Drought and conflict have resulted in massive population movement and displacement throughout the Horn. According to the United Nations, more than 100,000 people have fled from other parts of Somalia into Mogadishu.

Those who have been able to escape from Somalia take a harrowing journey through dry and insecure parts of southern Somalia, eastern Ethiopia and northern Kenya. Kenya has received about 130,000 new Somali arrivals since January, with 85,000 arriving since June. In Ethiopia, 120,000 Somali refugees have arrived in Dolo Ado, with 80,000 arriving this year. Over the last two weeks, thousands have begun to arrive in Yemen.

This rapid and massive increase in people arriving in both Kenya and Ethiopia has posed significant challenges to responding to need, and leaving humanitarian agencies struggling. Three existing refugee camps in Dadaab were originally built to house 90,000 people but the according to the United Nations, approximately 430,000 Somali refugees are currently living in and around Dadaab. After considerable delay, a fourth camp has been opened along with extension sites to an existing camp.

In Ethiopia's Dolo Ado region, new camps are being built. The state of health of those arriving in Dolo Ado continues to be extremely poor and there has recently been a worrying rise in deaths among children under the age of five, the main cause of which appears to be measles. Malnutrition, pneumonia and diarrhea are also causing high infant mortality rates and death in children.

UN agencies and NGOs are working around the clock to try to provide basic services in all these camps, but with the arrival of an additional 1,200 refugees a day in Dadaab and increasing numbers in Dolo Ado, it is an uphill battle. Steps must be taken to ensure these additional camps meet humanitarian standards, with improved coordination and safe transfer of refugees from one location to another. The massive influx of refugees is also causing considerable tension with the host communities over water, resources and land. These tensions must be addressed and a longterm solution to the situation in Dadaab must be found.

CHALLENGES TO RESPONSE

Perhaps the greatest challenge to ensuring that lives are saved and this crisis does not worsen is making sure that all actors involved, including national governments, the international community, United Nations agencies, NGOs and civil society organizations respond swiftly and appropriately to the immediate and longer-term needs by ensuring adequate emergency and development funding and access, improving coordination and being flexible.

1. *Funding:* Currently, $2.4 billion is required to cover immediate humanitarian needs. $1.4 billion has already been provided and the United States is the lead donor, having provided just over $600 million. Other donors have stepped up, including the African Union, Saudi Arabia and other non-traditional donors. Oxfam commends the United States for its leadership and early response to the drought. Secretary Clinton's announcement of $17 million three weeks ago and USAID Administrator Shah's announcement last week of $23 million are critical to the response and we hope that the US government will be able to continue responding generously as this crisis unfolds.

    Increased funding for emergency accounts should not come at the expense of other relief and development accounts that fight poverty and often help prevent the need for emergency spending in the first place. In addition to emergency assistance, more investment in long-term solutions is required.

    Feed the Future (FTF) is an important initiative in this regard, and Oxfam commends its comprehensive approach to investment in country-owned agriculture and food security plans that involve key stakeholders in planning and implementation. Agriculture and pastoralism provide critical livelihoods for the 237 million people in East Africa who live in rural areas. The agriculture sector (farming and livestock) is essential for food availability, livelihoods and economic development in the region. The sector comprises a significant portion of gross domestic product (GDP) in the Horn countries - 44.5 per cent in Ethiopia, 27.0 per cent in Kenya and 65.0 per cent in Somalia. Yet, globally, the share of official development assistance that supports agriculture has declined by 77 per cent, accounting for only 7 per cent of the total official development assistance today. From 2005-2008, agriculture assistance as a share of official development assistance was 6.12 per cent in Ethiopia, 6.88 per cent in Kenya, and a mere 0.87 per cent in Somalia.

National governments must also play a role in directing investments toward agriculture. Ethiopia and Kenya have agreed to direct 10% percent of national budgets to agriculture, however the lack of investment in livestock production in the region is particularly stark. In Ethiopia livestock production contributes 40% of agricultural GDP, but the government only allocated 0.3% of its budget to investment in livestock production, while in Kenya livestock provides 50% of agricultural GDP, but receives less than 1% of the budget.

It is critical that the United States maintain full funding for the emergency accounts and make greater investments in agriculture, disaster risk reduction and long-term development assistance, such as Feed the Future.

2. *Access:* Along with donor funding, access remains another significant challenge, especially in Somalia. South central Somalia is one of the world's most difficult environments to work in, yet Oxfam's partners continue to operate and provide services to the community. Additionally, donors have placed legal restrictions on international NGOs that have compounded their ability to adequately respond to the needs. As the United States continues to respond to the famine in Somalia and drought in the region, it is critical that humanitarian assistance is given on the basis of needs alone and that response remains neutral and impartial.

3. ***Coordination and Flexibility:*** The scale and scope of this emergency presents numerous challenges to the humanitarian response, and we need to ensure not only that enough money is provided, but also that it reaches those most in need. Therefore, coordination, information sharing and transparency amongst all actors must be improved. Now more than ever, humanitarian actors need to be strategic and flexible in how we provide assistance.

WAYS FORWARD

The Horn of Africa is highly vulnerable to natural hazards, particularly drought, and climate variability is expected to increase in the future, which will have major impacts on livelihoods and food production. Disaster Risk Reduction (DRR) seeks to analyse, manage and address the causal factors of disasters and their impact on men and women. DRR activities should be a core feature of humanitarian, rehabilitation and development programming going forward, because appropriate prevention not only saves lives but also money. Unfortunately there is a lack of priority given to resilience building, especially for poor farmers, in the region.

DRR funding represents a very small percentage of overall humanitarian and development activity expenditures. New global data shows slowly increasing expenditures, but still to only extremely low levels. Global expenditure on DRR in 2009 reached $835 million – a mere 0.5 per cent of total annual official development assistance.

Studies have shown the wisdom of investing in DRR. For example, protecting core livestock herds is much cheaper than rebuilding them once they have been decimated by drought. One study found that in northern Kenya, it was three times more expensive to restock a core herd than keep animals alive through supplementary feeding. In the Afar region of Ethiopia, restocking sheep and goats costs 6.5 times more than supplementary feeding, and restocking cattle costs 14 times more.

In Ethiopia, as a result of Oxfam America's disaster risk reduction programs to build and preserve livelihood assets, communities that received emergency aid in previous droughts are not in need of assistance. For example, a small-scale irrigation project developed in Liban district of Guji zone pumped water from a major river to enable pastoralist households to produce grain not only for their own consumption but also for local market supply. Women report that they no longer worry about milk and food shortages for their children and families. In contrast to last year and neighboring pastoralists' communities, this community is no longer included in food aid targeting and they have not been forced to migrate with their livestock, due to the lack of animal feed. Oxfam is seeing similar resilience being built through support for community grain banks and cattle restocking programs. Cash-for-food programs have helped communities in Ethiopia develop more than 2,000 hectares of degraded land into grasses for herds to graze. More than 15,000 pastoralist households with which Oxfam has been working with are still benefiting during the current drought from having preserved hay, now used for feeding dairy cows in a "cut and carry" management system.

Solutions do exist to ensure that crises on this scale are avoided. Governments and the international community need to treat this as a long-term problem as well as an urgent crisis. This is not a standalone emergency but a recurring problem that will become more severe and frequent. The chronic cycle of food insecurity is leaving donors and affected communities limping from one crisis to the next. It is a cycle that must be broken.

Recommendations to the US Government

- Use its influence to ensure a strong and strategic humanitarian response, where humanitarian principles are upheld, and actors are encouraged to share timely, accurate information about their activities, any challenges they may face or limitations to what they can do.
- Fully fund and maintain the emergency accounts to ensure as many lives are saved as possible, including support for cash-based interventions and other alternative programs.
- Invest a portion of humanitarian and development assistance towards disaster risk reduction and promote a global compact between development and humanitarian actors that would put disaster risk reduction at the heart of development approaches in disaster prone countries.
- Fully fund Feed the Future and ensure that USAID has the flexibility to re-assess and if necessary realign investment priorities, in consultation with developing country stakeholders, in the context of the current crisis.
- Fulfill the pledges made to the L'Aquila Food Security Initiative (AFSI) to fulfill the US piece of the L'Aquila commitment of $3.5 billion for agriculture and food security over three years. This should be seen as a down payment on a long-term commitment to funding agriculture and food security activities in a manner consistent with Feed the Future. Also should agree to a longer-term plan for fighting food insecurity and malnutrition after the AFSI expires in 2012.
- Support national governments in the establishment of social protection and safety net programs, such as delivering regular food, cash or vouchers, which will protect poor people from the impact of food crises, reduce and reverse malnutrition of vulnerable populations

including children under the age of five and encourage national governments and other donors to do the same.

- Make concrete commitments towards building the resilience and productivity of pastoralists and other small scale food producers, including policies and long-term investments that focus on drought cycle management; development of dry land areas and affected pastoral communities; improving access to markets for smallholders; targeted support to women and provision of financial services including savings, credit and insurance.

United States House of Representatives
Committee on Foreign Affairs

"TRUTH IN TESTIMONY" DISCLOSURE FORM

Clause 2(g) of rule XI of the Rules of the House of Representatives and the Rules of the Committee require the disclosure of the following information. A copy of this form should be attached to your written testimony and will be made publicly available in electronic format, per House Rules.

1. Name:	2. Organization or organizations you are representing:
SHANNON SCRIBNER	OXFAM AMERICA

3. Date of Committee hearing:

SEPTEMBER 8, 2011

4. Have you received any Federal grants or contracts (including any subgrants and subcontracts) since October 1, 2008 related to the subject on which you have been invited to testify?	5. Have any of the organizations you are representing received any Federal grants or contracts (including any subgrants and subcontracts) since October 1, 2008 related to the subject on which you have been invited to testify?
☐ Yes ☒ No	☐ Yes ☒ No

6. If you answered yes to either item 4 or 5, please list the source and amount of each grant or contract, and indicate whether the recipient of such grant was you or the organization(s) you are representing. You may list additional grants or contracts on additional sheets.

7. Signature:

Please attach a copy of this form to your written testimony.

In: Humanitarian Crisis and Response ...   ISBN: 978-1-61942-540-8
Editors: C.J. Newsome and H.I. Herron © 2012 Nova Science Publishers, Inc.

Chapter 9

SOMALIA COUNTRY PROFILE

United States Department of State

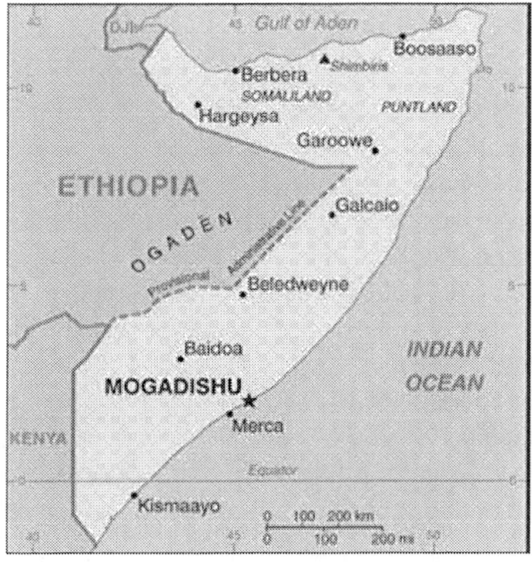

Flag of Somalia.

NOTE: There is no official U.S. representation in Somalia. Statistical data on Somalia in this report are subject to dispute and error.

GEOGRAPHY

Area: 637,657 sq. km.; slightly smaller than Texas.

Cities: Capital--Mogadishu. Other cities--Beledweyne, Kismayo, Baidoa, Jowhar, Merca, Gaalkayo, Bosasso, Hargeisa, Berbera.

Terrain: Mostly flat to undulating plateau rising to hills in the north.

Climate: Principally desert; December to February--northeast monsoon, moderate temperatures in north, and very hot in the south; May to October--southwest monsoon, torrid in the north, and hot in the south; irregular rainfall; hot and humid periods (tangambili) between monsoons.

PEOPLE

Nationality: Noun--Somali(s). Adjective--Somali.

Population (2011 est., no census exists): 9.9 million (of which an estimated 2 million in Somaliland).

Annual population growth rate (2011 est.): 1.6%.

Ethnic groups: Somali, with a small non-Somali minority (mostly Bantu and Arabs). Religion: 99.9% Muslim.

Languages: Somali (official), Arabic, Italian, English.

Education: Literacy--total population that can read and write, 37.8%: male 49.7%; female 25.8%.

Health: Infant mortality rate--109.19/1,000 live births. Life expectancy at birth--total population: 50.4 yrs.

Work force (3.4 million; very few are skilled workers): Pastoral nomad--60%. Agriculture, government, trading, fishing, industry, handicrafts, and other--40%.

GOVERNMENT

Type: Transitional government, known as the Transitional Federal Government (TFG).

Independence: July 1, 1960 (from a merger between the former Somaliland Protectorate under British rule, which became independent from the U.K. on June 26, 1960, and Italian Somaliland, which became independent from the Italian-administered UN trusteeship on July 1, 1960, to form the Somali Republic).

Constitution: None in force. Note: A Transitional Federal Charter was established in February 2004 and is expected to serve as the basis for a future constitution in Somalia.

Branches: Executive--TFG President, TFG Prime Minister, cabinet (Council of Ministers).

Legislative--Transitional Federal Parliament. Judicial--Supreme Court not functioning; no functioning nationwide legal system; informal legal system based on previously codified law, Islamic (shari'a) law, customary practices, and the provisions of the Transitional Federal Charter. Note: Two regional administrations exist in northern Somalia--the self-declared "Republic of Somaliland" in the northwest and the semi-autonomous state of Puntland in the northeast.

Political party: None.

Suffrage: 18 years of age; universal (no nationwide elections).

Administrative subdivisions: 18 regions (plural--NA; singular--Gobolka). Awdal, Bakool, Banaadir, Bari, Bay, Galguduud, Gedo, Hiraan, Jubbada Dhexe, Jubbada Hoose, Mudug, Nugaal, Sanaag, Shabeellaha Dhexe, Shabeellah Hoose, Sool, Togdheer, Woqooyi Galbeed. Central government budget: N/A.

Defense: N/A.

National holiday: July 1 (June 26 in Somaliland).

ECONOMY

GDP (2010 est.): U.S. $5.9 billion.

Annual growth rate (2010 est.): 2.6%.

Per capita GDP (2010 est.): $600.

Avg. inflation rate: N/A.

Natural resources: Largely unexploited reserves of iron ore, tin, gypsum, bauxite, uranium, copper, salt; likely petroleum and natural gas reserves.

Agriculture: Products--livestock, fish, bananas, corn, sorghum, sugar. Arable land--13%, of which 2% is cultivated.

Industry: Types--Telecommunications, livestock, fishing, textiles, transportation, limited financial services. Somalia's surprisingly innovative private sector has continued to function despite the lack of a functioning central government since 1991.

Trade: Exports--$300 million (f.o.b., 2010 est.): livestock, bananas, hides, fish, charcoal, scrap metal. Major markets--United Arab Emirates, Yemen, Saudi Arabia. Imports--$798 million (f.o.b., 2006 est.): food grains, animal and vegetable oils, petroleum products, construction materials, manufactured products, qat. Major suppliers--Djibouti, India, Kenya, United States, Oman, United Arab Emirates, Yemen.

Aid disbursed: N/A.

Remittances (2008 est.): $2 billion.

Geography

Somalia is located on the east coast of Africa and north of the Equator and, with Ethiopia, Eritrea, Djibouti, and Kenya, is often referred to as the Horn of Africa. It comprises Italy's former Trust Territory of Somalia and the former British Protectorate of Somaliland (now seeking recognition as an independent state). The coastline extends 2,720 kilometers (1,700 mi.).

The northern part of the country is hilly, and in many places the altitude ranges between 900 and 2,100 meters (3,000-7,000 ft.) above sea level. The central and southern areas are flat, with an average altitude of less than 180 meters (600 ft.). The Juba and the Shabelle Rivers rise in Ethiopia and flow south across the country toward the Indian Ocean. The Shabelle does not reach the sea.

Major climatic factors are a year-round hot climate, seasonal monsoon winds, and irregular rainfall with recurring droughts. Mean daily maximum temperatures range from 30°C to 40°C (85° F-105°F), except at higher elevations and along the east coast. Mean daily minimums usually vary from about 15°C to 30°C (60°F-85°F). The southwest monsoon, a sea breeze, makes the period from about May to October the mildest season in Somalia. The December-February period of the northeast monsoon also is relatively mild, although prevailing climatic conditions in Somalia are rarely pleasant. The "tangambili" periods that intervene between the two rainy seasons (October-November and March-May) are hot and humid.

People

The Cushitic populations of the Somali Coast in the Horn of Africa have an ancient history. Known by ancient Arabs as the Berberi, archaeological evidence indicates their presence in the Horn of Africa by A.D. 100 and possibly earlier. As early as the seventh century A.D., the indigenous Cushitic peoples began to mingle with Arab and Persian traders who had settled along the coast. Interaction over the centuries led to the emergence of a Somali culture bound by common traditions, a single language, and the Islamic faith.

The Somali-populated region of the Horn of Africa stretches from the Gulf of Tadjoura in modern-day Djibouti through Dire Dawa, Ethiopia, and down to the coastal regions of southern Kenya. Since gaining independence in 1960, the goal of Somali nationalism, also known as Pan-Somalism, has been the unification of all Somali populations, forming a Greater Somalia. This issue has been a major cause of past crises between Somalia and its neighbors--Ethiopia, Kenya, and Djibouti.

Today, about 60% of all Somalis are nomadic or semi-nomadic pastoralists who raise cattle, camels, sheep, and goats. About 25% of the population is settled farmers who live mainly in the fertile agricultural zone between the Juba and Shabelle Rivers in southern Somalia. The remainder of the population (approximately 15%) is urban.

Sizable ethnic groups in the country include Bantu agricultural workers, several thousand Arabs and some hundreds of Indians and Pakistanis. Nearly all inhabitants speak the Somali language. The language remained unwritten until October 1973, when the Supreme Revolutionary Council (SRC) proclaimed it the nation's official language and decreed an orthography using Latin letters. Somali is now the language of instruction in schools, although Arabic, English, and Italian also are used extensively.

History

Early history traces the development of the Somali state to an Arab sultanate, which was founded in the seventh century A.D. by Koreishite immigrants from Yemen. During the 15th and 16th centuries, Portuguese traders landed in present Somali territory and ruled several coastal towns. The sultan of Oman and Zanzibar subsequently took control of these towns and their surrounding territory.

Somalia's modern history began in the late 19th century, when various European powers began to trade and establish themselves in the area. The British East India Company's desire for unrestricted harbor facilities led to the conclusion of treaties with the sultan of Tajura as early as 1840. It was not until 1886, however, that the British gained control over northern Somalia through treaties with various Somali chiefs who were guaranteed British protection. British objectives centered on safeguarding trade links to the east and securing local sources of food and provisions for its coaling station in Aden. The boundary between Ethiopia and British Somaliland was established in 1897 through treaty negotiations between British negotiators and King Menelik.

During the first 2 decades of the 1900s, British rule was challenged through persistent attacks by a dervish rebellion led by Mohamed Abdullah, known as the "Mad Mullah" by the British. A long series of intermittent engagements and truces ended in 1920 when British warplanes bombed Abdullah's stronghold at Taleex. Although Abdullah was defeated as much by rival Somali factions as by British forces, he was lauded as a popular hero and stands as a major figure of national identity to many Somalis.

In 1885, Italy obtained commercial advantages in the area from the sultan of Zanzibar and in 1889 concluded agreements with the sultans of Obbia and Aluula, who placed their territories under Italy's protection. Between 1897 and 1908, Italy made agreements with the Ethiopians and the British that marked out the boundaries of Italian Somaliland. The Italian Government assumed direct administration, giving the territory colonial status.

Italian occupation gradually extended inland. In 1924, the Jubaland Province of Kenya, including the town and port of Kismayo, was ceded to Italy by the United Kingdom. The subjugation and occupation of the independent sultanates of Obbia and Mijertein, begun in 1925, were completed in 1927. In the late 1920s, Italian and Somali influence expanded into the Ogaden region of eastern Ethiopia. Continuing incursions climaxed in 1935 when Italian forces launched an offensive that led to the capture of Addis Ababa and the Italian annexation of Ethiopia in 1936.

Following Italy's declaration of war on the United Kingdom in June 1940, Italian troops overran British Somaliland and drove out the British garrison. In 1941, British forces began operations against the Italian East African Empire and quickly brought the greater part of Italian Somaliland under British control. From 1941 to 1950, while Somalia was under British military administration, transition toward self-government was begun through the establishment of local courts, planning committees, and the Protectorate

Advisory Council. In 1948, Britain turned the Ogaden and neighboring Somali territories over to Ethiopia.

In Article 23 of the 1947 peace treaty, Italy renounced all rights and titles to Italian Somaliland. In accordance with treaty stipulations, on September 15, 1948, the Four Powers referred the question of disposal of former Italian colonies to the UN General Assembly. On November 21, 1949, the General Assembly adopted a resolution recommending that Italian Somaliland be placed under an international trusteeship system for 10 years, with Italy as the administering authority, followed by independence for Italian Somaliland. In 1959, at the request of the Somali Government, the UN General Assembly advanced the date of independence from December 2 to July 1, 1960.

Meanwhile, rapid progress toward self-government was being made in British Somaliland. Elections for the Legislative Assembly were held in February 1960, and one of the first acts of the new legislature was to request that the United Kingdom grant the area independence so that it could be united with Italian Somaliland when the latter became independent. The protectorate became independent on June 26, 1960; 5 days later, on July 1, it joined Italian Somaliland to form the Somali Republic.

In June 1961, Somalia adopted its first national constitution in a countrywide referendum, which provided for a democratic state with a parliamentary form of government based on European models. During the early post-independence period, political parties were a fluid concept, with one-person political parties forming before an election, only to defect to the winning party following the election. A constitutional conference in Mogadishu in April 1960, which made the system of government in the southern Somali trust territory the basis for the future government structure of the Somali Republic, resulted in the concentration of political power in the former Italian Somalia capital of Mogadishu and a southern-dominated central government. Most key government positions were occupied by southern Somalis, producing increased disenchantment with the union in the former British-controlled north. Pan-Somali nationalism, with the goal of uniting the Somali-populated regions of French Somaliland (Djibouti), Kenya, and Ethiopia into a Greater Somalia remained the driving political ideology in the initial post-independence period. Under the leadership of Mohamed Ibrahim Egal (prime minister from 1967 to 1969), however, Somalia renounced its claims to the Somali-populated regions of Ethiopia and Kenya, greatly improving its relations with both countries. Egal's move towards reconciliation with Ethiopia, which had been a traditional enemy of Somalia since the 16th century, made many Somalis furious, including the army. This reconciliation effort is argued to be one of the principal factors that provoked a bloodless coup on October 21, 1969 and subsequent installation of Maj. Gen. Mohamed Siad Barre as president, bringing an abrupt end to the process of party-based constitutional democracy in Somalia.

Following the coup, executive and legislative power was vested in the 20-member Supreme Revolutionary Council (SRC), headed by Barre. The SRC pursued a course of "scientific socialism" that reflected both ideological and economic dependence on the Soviet Union. The government instituted a national security service, centralized control over information, and initiated a number of grassroots development projects. Barre reduced political freedoms and used military force to seize and redistribute rich farmlands in the areas of southern Somalia between the Juba and Shabelle Rivers, relying on the use of force and terror against the Somali population to consolidate his political power base.

The SRC became increasingly radical in foreign affairs, and in 1974, Somalia and the Soviet Union concluded a treaty of friendship and cooperation. As early as 1972, tensions began increasing along the Somali-Ethiopian border; these tensions heightened after the accession to power in Ethiopia in 1973 of the Mengistu Haile Mariam regime, which turned increasingly toward the Soviet Union. In the mid-1970s, the Western Somali Liberation Front (WSLF) began guerrilla operations in the Ogaden region of Ethiopia. Following the overthrow of the Ethiopian Emperor in 1975, Somalia invaded Ethiopia in 1977 in a second attempt to regain the Ogaden, and the second attempt initially appeared to be in Somalia's favor. The SNA moved quickly toward Harer, Jijiga, and Dire Dawa, the principal cities of the region. However, following the Ethiopian revolution, the new Ethiopian Government shifted its alliance from the West to the Soviet Union. Because of the new alliance, the Soviet Union supplied Ethiopia with 10,000-15,000 Cuban troops and Soviet military advisors during the 1977-78 Ogaden war, shifting the advantage to Ethiopia and resulting in Somalia's defeat. In November 1977, Barre expelled all Soviet advisers and abrogated the friendship agreement with the U.S.S.R. In March 1978, Somali forces retreated into Somalia; however, the WSLF continued to carry out sporadic but greatly reduced guerrilla activity in the Ogaden. Such activities also were subsequently undertaken by another dissident group, the Ogaden National Liberation Front (ONLF).

Following the Ogaden war, desperate to find a strong external alliance to replace the Soviet Union, Somalia abandoned its Socialist ideology and turned to the West for international support, military equipment, and economic aid. In 1978, the United States reopened the U.S. Agency for International

Development mission in Somalia. Two years later, an agreement was concluded that gave U.S. forces access to military facilities at the port of Berbera in northwestern Somalia. In the summer of 1982, Ethiopian forces invaded Somalia along the central border, and the United States provided two emergency airlifts to help Somalia defend its territorial integrity. From 1982 to 1988, the United States viewed Somalia as a partner in defense in the context of the Cold War. Somali officers of the National Armed Forces were trained in U.S. military schools in civilian as well as military subjects.

During this time, the Barre regime violently suppressed opposition movements and ethnic groups, particularly the Isaaq clan in the northern region, using the military and elite security forces to quash any hint of rebellion. By the 1980s, an all-out civil war developed in Somalia. Opposition groups began to form following the end of the Ogaden war, beginning in 1979 with a group of dissatisfied army officers known as the Somali Salvation Democratic Front (SSDF). In 1981, as a result of increased northern discontent with the Barre regime, the Somali National Movement (SNM), composed mainly of the Isaaq clan, was formed in Hargeisa with the stated goal of overthrowing of the Barre regime. In January 1989, the United Somali Congress (USC), an opposition group of Somalis from the Hawiye clan, was formed as a political movement in Rome. A military wing of the USC was formed in Ethiopia in late 1989 under the leadership of Mohamed Farah "Aideed," a former political prisoner imprisoned by Barre from 1969-75. Aideed also formed alliances with other opposition groups, including the SNM and the Somali Patriotic Movement (SPM), an Ogadeen sub-clan force under Colonel Ahmed Omar Jess in the Bakool and Bay regions of Southern Somalia. In 1988, at the President's order, aircraft from the Somali National Air Force bombed the city of Hargeisa in northwestern Somalia, the former capital of British Somaliland, killing nearly 10,000 civilians and insurgents. The warfare in the northwest sped up the decay already evident elsewhere in the republic. Economic crisis, brought on by the cost of anti-insurgency activities, caused further hardship as Siad Barre and his cronies looted the national treasury.

By the end of the 1980s, armed opposition to Barre's government, fully operational in the northern regions, had spread to the central and southern regions. Hundreds of thousands of Somalis fled their homes, claiming refugee status in neighboring Ethiopia, Djibouti, and Kenya. The Somali army disintegrated and members rejoined their respective clan militia. Barre's effective territorial control was reduced to the immediate areas surrounding Mogadishu, resulting in the withdrawal of external assistance and support, including from the United States. By the end of 1990, the Somali state was in the final stages of complete collapse. In the first week of December 1990, Barre declared a state of emergency as USC and SNM forces advanced toward Mogadishu. In January 1991, armed opposition factions drove Barre out of power, resulting in the complete collapse of the central government. Barre later died in exile in Nigeria. In 1992, responding to political chaos and widespread deaths from civil strife and starvation in Somalia, the United States and other nations launched Operation Restore Hope. Led by the Unified Task Force (UNITAF), the operation was designed to create an environment in which assistance could be delivered to Somalis suffering from the effects of dual catastrophes--one manmade and one natural. UNITAF was followed by the United Nations Operation in Somalia (UNOSOM). The United States played a major role in both operations. On October 3-4, 1993, 18 U.S. servicemen were killed in an incident made famous by the book and movie "Black Hawk Down." The United States continued operations until March 25, 1994, when U.S. forces withdrew.

Following the collapse of the Barre regime in 1991, various groupings of Somali factions sought to control the national territory (or portions thereof) and fought small wars with one another. Approximately 14 national reconciliation conferences were convened over the succeeding decade. Efforts at mediation of the Somali internal dispute were also undertaken by many regional states. In the mid-1990s, Ethiopia played host to several Somali peace conferences and initiated talks at the Ethiopian city of Sodere, which led to some degree of agreement between competing factions. The Governments of Egypt, Yemen, Kenya, and Italy also have attempted to bring the Somali factions together. In 1997, the Organization of African Unity and the Intergovernmental Authority on Development (IGAD) gave Ethiopia the mandate to pursue Somali reconciliation. In 2000, Djibouti hosted a major reconciliation conference (the 13th such effort), which in August resulted in creation of the Transitional National Government (TNG), whose 3-year mandate expired in August 2003. Kenya organized the Somalia National Reconciliation Conference, a 14th reconciliation effort, in 2002 under IGAD auspices. The conference concluded in August 2004 with the establishment of a Transitional Federal Government (TFG).

The absence of a central government in Somalia allowed outside forces to become more influential by supporting various groups and persons in Somalia, particularly Djibouti, Eritrea, Ethiopia, Egypt, Yemen, and Libya, all of which have supported various Somali factions and transitional governments. In July 2006, Ethiopian forces invaded Somalia and defeated the Islamic Courts

Union (ICU). In January 2009, Ethiopian forces completely withdrew from Somalia. U.S.-designated foreign terrorist organization al-Shabaab, formerly the military wing nominally under the ICU, became independent of the Courts and launched a multi-faction insurgency after the Courts scattered as a result of the 2006 invasion. Al-Shabaab and other extremist forces garnered power in subsequent years through their effective fighting of the Ethiopians, intimidation, and harsh implementation of shari'a law. Up until an anti-al-Shabaab offensive began in the western regions of southern Somalia in early 2011, al-Shabaab had controlled much of south central Somalia and parts of Mogadishu. Responding to a crushing famine in the south central region and recent setbacks at the hands of the TFG and AMISON, al-Shabaab largely pulled out of Mogadishu in August 2011. While al-Shabaab's violent attacks continue to limit the TFG's ability to provide public services, as well as prevent the delivery of humanitarian aid to vulnerable Somali populations, al-Shabaab does not enjoy as wide-reaching control as in late 2010.

Beginning in spring 2011, Somalia and the greater Horn of Africa experienced what some have called the worst drought in 60 years. Massive crop failure and a drastic rise in food prices coupled with the security situation in al-Shabaab controlled areas of south and central Somalia led the UN to declare famine in six areas. To date, 4 million Somalis are in need of emergent famine assistance and 750,000 are in danger of dying. This famine has forced thousands of Somalis into already stretched refugee camps in Ethiopia, Kenya, and Djibouti, while others have fled to IDP camps in Mogadishu. Al-Shabaab continues to deny international aid to the most affected communities. The United States, UN, and international humanitarian agencies have been working to address both the immediate needs of the Somali people and work toward a more permanent solution to stop similar crises in Somalia.

Piracy

The lack of governance and resulting instability led to the emergence of Somalia-based maritime piracy in the form of hijacking vessels and their crews for ransoms. Since 2008, the number of attacks annually by Somali pirates has risen into the hundreds and spread beyond the immediate coast of Somalia as far away as the Gulf of Oman and the western Indian Ocean. The UN Security Council has passed a series of resolutions authorizing states to undertake all necessary measures in Somalia to suppress acts of piracy. In January 2009, the Contact Group on Piracy off the Coast of Somalia was established to coordinate international counter-piracy efforts, including the multinational naval task forces conducting patrols and escort operations off the coast of Somalia to protect international shipping lines. With average ransom payments for hijacked ships reaching several million U.S. dollars, piracy has developed into a complex and lucrative economy of its own with negative impacts on global commerce, regional security, and Somali society, particularly in the states of Puntland and Galmudug, where most pirate attacks from Somalia are based.

GOVERNMENT AND POLITICAL CONDITIONS

In early 2002, Kenya organized a reconciliation effort under IGAD auspices known as the Somalia National Reconciliation Conference, which concluded in October 2004. A transitional government, the components of which are known as the Transitional Federal Institutions (TFIs), was formed in accordance with the Transitional Federal Charter. The TFIs include a transitional parliament, known as the Transitional Federal Parliament (TFP), as well as a Transitional Federal Government (TFG) that includes a transitional president, prime minister, and a cabinet known as the "Council of Ministers." For administrative purposes, Somalia is divided into 18 regions; the nature, authority, and structure of regional governments vary, where they exist.

The TFG was established with a 5-year mandate leading to the establishment of a permanent government following national elections in 2009. In January 2009, the TFP extended this mandate an additional 2 years to 2011 and expanded to include 200 members of Parliament (MPs) from the opposition Alliance for the Reliberation of Somalia and 75 MPs from civil society and other groups, doubling the size of the TFP to 550 MPs. Consideration of a constitution continues.

Abdullahi Yusuf Ahmed was elected president of the TFG of Somalia on October 10, 2004. Sheikh Adan Mohamed Nur "Madobe" was elected speaker of the Parliament on January 31, 2007. President Abdullahi Yusuf Ahmed resigned on December 29, 2008, and Sheikh Sharif Sheikh Ahmed was elected by the Parliament as TFG President on January 30, 2009. On February 13, 2009, President Sharif appointed Omar Abdirashid Ali Sharmarke as the new prime minister of the TFG, and Sharmarke was confirmed by the TFP on February 14. A new cabinet of 36 ministers was appointed on February 20, 2009, and approved by Parliament on February 21, 2009. Prime Minister

Sharmarke restructured his cabinet on August 18, 2009, appointing several new ministers, including the ministers of foreign affairs and defense, and creating several new posts. This shake-up brought the number of ministers to 39. On March 15, 2010, the TFG signed an agreement with the militia group Ahlu-sunah Wal-jamea (ASWJ) bringing ASWJ into the TFG. After growing conflict with the President, Sharmarke resigned as prime minister on September 21, 2010 following disagreement over the draft constitution and other issues. Mohamed Abdullahi Mohamed, a Somali American, was confirmed as the new prime minister on November 8, with a confidence vote of 297 to 92 in Parliament.

In February 2011, the TFG unilaterally extended its mandate by 3 years, from August 2011 to August 2014, without consultation with the international community. The international community almost unanimously opposed this action due to the absence of a TFG roadmap for securing the end of the transition and completing the transitional tasks outlined in the Djibouti Peace Agreement, and the lack of projected governance reforms. To resolve the political impasse surrounding the unilateral extension of its mandate, the TFG agreed in June 2011 to extend its mandate for 12 months as part of the Kampala Accord. This accord consigned the TFG to finish its transitional tasks and set up a permanent government by August 2012. On September 6, 2011, the TFG and representatives from Puntland, Galmudug, and the ASWJ signed the "Roadmap to End the Transition" toward political reform in anticipation of the end of the TFG's extended mandate in 2012. This Roadmap set forward goals like working toward a permanent constitution, holding elections, and reforming Somalia's 550-member parliament.

Two regional administrations exist in northern Somalia--the self-declared "Republic of Somaliland" in the northwest and the semi-autonomous state of Puntland in the northeast. Several nascent regional authorities central Somalia—Galmudug, Himan iyo Heeb, and ASWJ-controlled territory—have maintained relative peace and order since 2011.

In 1991, a congress drawn from the inhabitants of the former Somaliland Protectorate declared withdrawal from the 1960 union with Somalia to form the self-declared "Republic of Somaliland." Somaliland has not received international recognition, but has maintained a de jure separate status since that time. Its form of government is republican, with a bicameral legislature including an elected elders chamber and a house of representatives. The judiciary is independent, and three official political parties exist. In line with the Somaliland Constitution, Vice President Dahir Riyale Kahin assumed the presidency following the death of former President Mohamed Ibrahim Egal in

2002. Kahin was elected President of Somaliland in elections determined to be free and fair by international observers in May 2003. Elections for the 84-member lower house of parliament took place on September 29, 2005 and were described as transparent and credible by international observers. Somaliland held its next presidential elections in June 2010. President Ahmed Mohamed Mohamoud Silanyo (President Silanyo) was elected.

The area of Puntland declared itself autonomous (although not independent) in 1998 with its capital at Garoowe. President Abdirahman Mohamed Farole was elected by the Puntland parliament in January 2009. Puntland declared it would remain autonomous until a federated Somalia state was established.

Principal Government Officials

President--Sheikh Sharif Sheikh Ahmed
Prime Minister--Mohamed Abdullahi Mohamed
Speaker of Parliament—Sharif Hassan Sheik Aden

Ministers

Prime Minister's Office--Sahra Mohamed Ali Samantar
Office of the President--Abdiqadir Moalin Nuur
Foreign Affairs--Mohamed Abdullahi Omar
Finance and Treasury—Hussain Abdi Halane
Defense—Abdihakim Mahamud Hajji Fiqi
Interior and National Security—Abdishakku Sheik Hasan Farah
Fisheries and Marine Resources--Mohamed Malin Hasan
Ports, Water, Air, and Land Transport—Ahmed Abdirahman Abade
Health—Adan Hajji Ibrahim Daud

Deputy Ministers

Justice and Religious Affairs--Haji Ali Sheikh Mohamed
Foreign Affairs--Omar Sheikh Ali Idiris
Interior and National Security--Ibrahim Issak Yarow
Finance and Treasury--Muktar Sheikh Sufi Sheikh Cali

Defense--Daud Abdikarim Hashi Omar

Planning and Regional Cooperation--Abdiaziz Hassan Mohame "Lafta Garen"

Information, Post, and Telecommunication--Mohamed Ali Farah Gedi

Commerce and Industry--Mohamed Ali Shire Labor,

Development, and Social Affairs--Abdirashid Mohamed Hiddig

Public Works and Reconstruction--Abdi Ali Mohamed

Agriculture and Livestock Development--Hassan Yakub

Fisheries and Marine Resources--Abdullahi Abukar Jama

Ports, Water, Air, and Land Transport--Abdikadir Haji Mohamed Suldan

Constitution, Federalism, and Reconciliation--Said Mohamed Jimale

Minerals, Water, and Energy--Abdirahim Yusuf Farah

Education, Culture, and Higher Education--Feisal Omar Guled

Women and Family Affairs--Fatuma Hassan Ali

Health--Osman Libah Ibrahim

Permanent Representative to the United Nations--Elmi Ahmed Duale

Special Envoy to the United States—Abukar Arman

The self-declared "Republic of Somaliland" consists of a regional authority based in the city of Hargeisa, including a president, vice president, parliament, and cabinet officials.

The semi-autonomous state of Puntland has a regional government based in the city of Garoowe and includes a president, vice president, cabinet, and House of Representatives.

Economy

Somalia lacks natural resources and faces major development challenges. Recent economic reverses have left its people increasingly dependent on remittances from abroad. Its economy is pastoral and agricultural, with livestock--principally camels, cattle, sheep, and goats--representing the main form of wealth. Livestock exports in recent years have been severely reduced by periodic bans, ostensibly for concerns of animal health, by Arabian Peninsula states. Drought has also impaired agricultural and livestock production. Because rainfall is scanty and irregular, farming generally is limited to certain coastal districts, areas near Hargeisa, and the Juba and Shabelle River valleys. The agricultural sector of the economy consists mainly of banana plantations located in the south, which use modern irrigation systems and up-to-date farm machinery.

A small fishing industry exists in the north where tuna, shark, and other warm-water fish are caught, although fishing production is seriously affected by poaching. Aromatic woods--frankincense and myrrh--from a small and diminishing forest also contribute to the country's exports. Minerals, including uranium and likely deposits of petroleum and natural gas, are found throughout the country, but have not been exploited commercially. Petroleum exploration efforts have ceased due to insecurity and instability. Illegal production in the south of charcoal for export has led to widespread deforestation. With the help of foreign aid, small industries such as textiles, handicrafts, meat processing, and printing are being established.

The absence of central government authority, as well as profiteering from counterfeiting, has rapidly debased Somalia's currency. The self-declared "Republic of Somaliland" issues its own currency, the Somaliland shilling, which is not accepted outside of the self-declared republic.

There are no railways in Somalia; internal transportation is limited to truck and bus. The national road system nominally comprises 22,100 kilometers (13,702 mi.) of roads that include about 2,600 kilometers (1,612 mi.) of all-weather roads, although most roads have received little maintenance for years and have seriously deteriorated.

Air transportation is provided by small air charter firms. A number of airlines operate from Hargeisa. Some private airlines, including Daallo Airlines, serve several domestic locations as well as Djibouti and the United Arab Emirates. The UN and other nongovernmental organizations (NGOs) operate air service for their missions.

The European Community and the World Bank jointly financed construction of a deepwater port at Mogadishu. The Soviet Union improved Somalia's deepwater port at Berbera in 1969. Facilities at Berbera were further improved by a U.S. military construction program completed in 1985, but they have since become dilapidated. During the 1990s the United States renovated a deepwater port at Kismayo that serves the fertile Juba River basin and is vital to Somalia's banana export industry. Smaller ports are located at Merca, Brava, and Bossaso. Absence of security and lack of maintenance and improvement are major issues at most Somali ports.

Cellular phone service is readily available throughout the country, but landline communication systems have been destroyed or dismantled. Somalia is linked to the outside world via ship-to-shore communications (INMARSAT) as well as links to overseas satellite operators by private telecommunications operators (including cellular telephone systems) in major towns. Radio broadcasting stations operate at Mogadishu, Hargeisa, and Galkaiyo, with programs in Somali and some other languages. There are two television broadcast stations in Mogadishu and one in Hargeisa.

DEFENSE

The TFG controls several thousand trained army soldiers. Other various TFG-allied groups throughout Somalia are estimated to control militias ranging in strength from hundreds to thousands. The TFG and some groups possess limited inventories of older armored vehicles and other heavy weapons, and small arms are prevalent throughout Somalia. On September 8, 2009, 500 naval recruits graduated to form Somalia's first naval force in over 2 decades. The TFG plans to use the force to combat piracy off Somalia's coastline.

AMISOM

The United States has been a strong supporter of the African Union Mission in Somalia (AMISOM) since its deployment to Mogadishu in March 2007. As of October 2010, AMISOM consisted of over 8,000 peacekeepers from Uganda and Burundi. AMISOM plays a critical role in supporting the Djibouti Peace Process by protecting Transitional Federal Institutions and TFG personnel, and by securing critical infrastructure in Mogadishu, including the airport and the seaport.

As of October 2010, the U.S. Government had obligated over $258 million to support AMISOM with equipment, logistical support, and peacekeeping training. U.S. equipment support has included armored personnel carriers, trucks, communications equipment, water purification devices, generators, tents, and night vision equipment. Logistical support has included airlift, food, fuel, medical supplies, and medical evacuation flights. The U.S. Government has provided peacekeeping training to the Ugandan and Burundian peacekeepers through the Department of State's Africa Contingency Operations Training and Assistance (ACOTA) program.

In January 2009, the UN Security Council passed Resolution 1863, which called on the United Nations to establish a logistics support package for AMISOM. By October 2009, the United States had transferred most logistics support tasks (including the provision of food, fuel, and medical evacuation flights) to the UN Support Office for AMISOM (UNSOA), which the UN established to implement the logistics support package. The United States supports UNSOA and the logistics support package through its assessed contributions to the United Nations.

FOREIGN RELATIONS

Somalia followed a foreign policy of nonalignment for a brief period following independence. In 1970, the Siad Barre regime declared a national ideology based on scientific Socialism and aligned its foreign policy with the Soviet Union and China. In the 1980s, Somalia shifted its alignment to the West following a territorial conflict with Ethiopia over the disputed Somali-populated region of the Ogaden from 1977-78, in which the Soviet Union supported Ethiopia. The Somalia central government also sought ties with many Arab countries, and continued to receive financial and military support from several Arab countries prior to its collapse in 1991.

In 1963, Somalia severed diplomatic relations with the United Kingdom for a period following a dispute over Kenya's Somali-populated northeastern region (Northern Frontier District), an area inhabited mainly by Somalis. Related problems have arisen from the boundary with Ethiopia and the large-scale migrations of Somali nomads between Ethiopia and Somalia. In the aftermath of the 1977-78 war between Somalia and Ethiopia, the Government of Somalia continued to call for self-determination for ethnic Somalis living in the Ogaden region of eastern Ethiopia. At the March 1983 Nonaligned Movement summit in New Delhi, President Siad Barre stated that Somalia harbored no expansionist aims and was willing to negotiate with Ethiopia over the disputed Ogaden region.

Following the collapse of the Barre regime, the foreign policy of the various entities in Somalia, including the TFG, has centered on gaining international recognition, winning international support for national reconciliation, and obtaining international economic assistance.

U.S.-SOMALI RELATIONS

Although the United States never formally severed diplomatic relations with Somalia, the U.S. Embassy in Somalia has been closed since the collapse of the Siad Barre government in 1991. The United States maintains regular dialogue with the TFG and other key stakeholders in Somalia through the U.S. Embassy in Nairobi, Kenya. Consular coverage for Somalia is maintained by U.S. Embassy Nairobi, while American Citizens Services in the self-declared "Republic of Somaliland" are provided by the U.S. Embassy in Djibouti.

In: Humanitarian Crisis and Response ...   ISBN: 978-1-61942-540-8
Editors: C.J. Newsome and H.I. Herron © 2012 Nova Science Publishers, Inc.

Chapter 10

KENYA COUNTRY PROFILE

United States Department of State

Official Name: Republic of Kenya

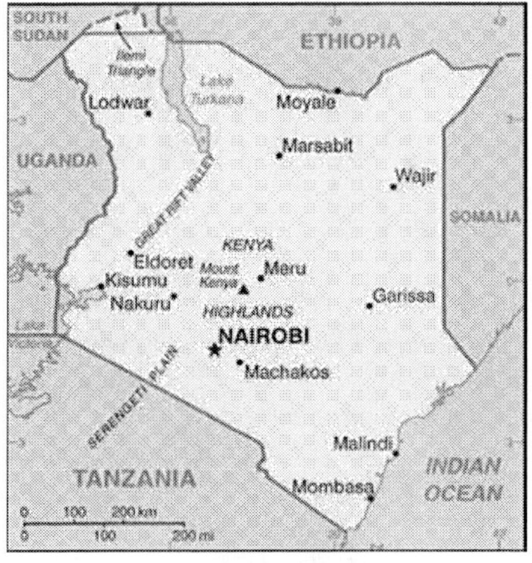

Flag of Kenya.

GEOGRAPHY

Area: 580,367 sq. km. (224,080 sq mi.); slightly smaller than Texas.

Cities: Cities: Capital--Nairobi (pop. 2.9 million; 2007 est.). *Other cities--*Mombasa (828,500; 2006 est.), Kisumu (650,846; 2005-6), Nakuru (1.3 million; 2005-6), Eldoret (193,830; 1999).

Terrain: Kenya rises from a low coastal plain on the Indian Ocean in a series of mountain ridges and plateaus which stand above 3,000 meters (9,000 ft.) in the center of the country. The Rift Valley bisects the country above Nairobi, opening up to a broad arid plain in the north. Highlands cover the south before descending to the shores of Lake Victoria in the west.

Climate: Tropical in south, west, and central regions; arid and semi-arid in the north and the northeast.

PEOPLE

Nationality: *Noun and adjective*--Kenyan(s).

Population (August 2010 est.): 39 million.

Major ethnic groups: Kikuyu 6.6 million, Luhya 5.3 million, Luo 4 million, Kalenjin 5 million, Kamba 3.9 million, Kisii 2.2 million, Mijikenda 1.9 million.

Religions: Christian 82.6%, Muslim 11.2%, traditional African religions 5%, Hindu/Sikh/Baha'i/Jewish 1%.

Languages: English (official), Swahili (national), over 40 other languages from the Bantu, Nilotic, and Cushitic linguistic groups.

Education: First 8 years of primary school are provided tuition-free by the government. In January 2008, the government began offering a program of free secondary education, subject to some restrictions. *Attendance--*92% for primary grades. *Adult literacy rate--*74%.

Health: *Infant mortality rate--*57.4/1,000. *Life expectancy--*55.3 yrs (2007 est.).

GOVERNMENT

Type: Republic.

Independence: December 12, 1963.

Constitution: 1963; new constitution approved in an August 4, 2010 referendum.

Branches: Executive--president (chief of state, commander in chief of armed forces), prime minister (head of government), and two deputy prime ministers. Legislative--unicameral National Assembly (parliament). Judicial--Supreme Court, Court of Appeal, High Court, various lower and special courts, including Kadhi (Sharia) courts.

Administrative subdivisions: 140 districts, joined to form 7 rural provinces. The Nairobi area has special provincial status. Under the new constitution, which is in the process of being implemented, the primary administrative subdivisions will be 47 counties, each with an elected governor.

Political party: Over 40 registered political parties. Two coalitions, the Party of National Unity (PNU) and the Orange Democratic Movement (ODM), dominate the political party scene. PNU membership is filled by parties representing Kikuyu and closely related ethnic groups; ODM membership ranks are filled by parties representing nearly everybody else. PNU and ODM agreed in February 2008 to form a coalition government in a power-sharing arrangement that ended the political crisis erupting after disputed national elections in December 2007. Suffrage: Universal at 18.

Economy

GDP (2010 est.): $32 billion.
Annual growth rate (2010): 5.4%.
Gross national income per capita (2008, Atlas Method): $780.
Natural resources: Wildlife, soda ash, land.
Agriculture: *Products*--tea, coffee, sugarcane, horticultural products, corn, wheat, rice, sisal, pineapples, pyrethrum, dairy products, meat and meat products, hides, skins. *Arable land*--17%.
Industry: *Types*--petroleum products, grain and sugar milling, cement, beer, soft drinks, textiles, vehicle assembly, paper and light manufacturing.
Structure of economy (% of GDP): *Services*--59.5%; *industry and commerce*--16.7%; *agriculture*--23.8%.
Work force: *Formal sector wage earners*--1.95 million (public sector 30%; private sector 70%). *Informal sector workers*--6.4 million.
Trade (FY 2010): *Exports*--$4.96 billion: tea, horticultural products, coffee, petroleum products, cement, pyrethrum, soda ash, sisal, hides and skins, fluorspar. *Major export markets*--Uganda, United Kingdom, Tanzania,

Netherlands, United States, Pakistan. *Imports*--$11.6 billion: machinery, vehicles, crude petroleum, iron and steel, resins and plastic materials, refined petroleum products, pharmaceuticals, paper and paper products, fertilizers, wheat. *Major suppliers*--United Arab Emirates, China, India, South Africa, Japan, United States.

People

Kenya has a very diverse population that includes three of Africa's major sociolinguistic groups: Bantu (67%), Nilotic (30%), and Cushitic (3%). Kenyans are deeply religious. About 80% of Kenyans are Christian, 11% Muslim, and the remainder follow traditional African religions or other faiths. Most city residents retain links with their rural, extended families and leave the city periodically to help work on the family farm. About 75% of the work force is engaged in agriculture, mainly as subsistence farmers. The national motto of Kenya is *Harambee*, meaning "pull together." In that spirit, volunteers in hundreds of communities build schools, clinics, and other facilities each year and collect funds to send students abroad.

Kenya has six full-pledged public universities: University of Nairobi, Jomo Kenyatta University of Agriculture and Technology, Egerton University, Moi University, Maseno University, Masinde Muliro University (most of these universities also have constituent colleges); and approximately 13 private universities, including United States International University. Public and private universities have a total enrollment of approximately 50,000 students with about 80% of these being enrolled in public universities (representing 25% of students who qualify for university admission). In addition, more than 60,000 students enroll in middle-level colleges where they study career courses leading to certificate, diploma, and higher diploma awards. International universities and colleges have also established campuses in Kenya where students enroll for distance learning and other flexible programs. Other Kenyan students pursue their university education abroad. More than 5,000 Kenyans are studying in the United States.

History

Fossils found in East Africa suggest that protohumans roamed the area more than 20 million years ago. Recent finds near Kenya's Lake Turkana indicate that hominids lived in the area 2.6 million years ago.

Cushitic-speaking people from what became Sudan, South Sudan, and Ethiopia moved into the area that is now Kenya beginning around 2000 BC. Arab traders began frequenting the Kenya coast around the first century AD. Kenya's proximity to the Arabian Peninsula invited colonization, and Arab and Persian settlements sprouted along the coast by the eighth century. During the first millennium AD, Nilotic and Bantu peoples moved into the region, and the latter now comprise two thirds of Kenya's population. Swahili, a Bantu language with significant Arabic vocabulary, developed as a trade language for the region.

Arab dominance on the coast was interrupted for about 150 years following the arrival of the Portuguese in 1498. British exploration of East Africa in the mid-1800s eventually led to the establishment of Britain's East African Protectorate in 1895. The Protectorate promoted settlement of the fertile central highlands by Europeans, dispossessing the Kikuyu and others of their land. Some fertile and well watered parts of the Rift Valley inhabited by the Maasai and the western highlands inhabited by the Kalenjin were also handed over to European settlers. For other Kenyan communities, the British presence was slight, especially in the arid northern half of the country. The settlers were allowed a voice in government even before Kenya was officially made a British colony in 1920, but Africans were prohibited from direct political participation until 1944 when a few appointed (but not elected) African representatives were permitted to sit in the legislature.

From 1952 to 1959, Kenya was under a state of emergency arising from the "Mau Mau" insurgency against British colonial rule in general and its land policies in particular. This rebellion took place almost exclusively in the highlands of central Kenya among the Kikuyu people. Tens of thousands of Kikuyu died in the fighting or in the detention camps and restricted villages. British losses were about 650. During this period, African participation in the political process increased rapidly.

The first direct elections for Africans to the Legislative Council took place in 1957. Kenya became independent on December 12, 1963, and the next year joined the Commonwealth. Jomo Kenyatta, an ethnic Kikuyu and head of the Kenya African National Union (KANU), became Kenya's first President. The minority party, Kenya African Democratic Union (KADU), representing a coalition of small ethnic groups that had feared dominance by larger ones, dissolved itself in 1964 and joined KANU.

A small but significant leftist opposition party, the Kenya People's Union (KPU), was formed in 1966, led by Jaramogi Oginga Odinga, a former Vice President and Luo elder. The KPU was banned shortly thereafter, however, and its leader detained. KANU became Kenya's sole political party. At Kenyatta's death in August 1978, Vice President Daniel arap Moi, a Kalenjin from Rift Valley province, became interim President. By October of that year, Moi became President formally after he was elected head of KANU and designated its sole nominee for the presidential election.

In June 1982, the National Assembly amended the constitution, making Kenya officially a one-party state. Two months later, young military officers in league with some opposition elements attempted to overthrow the government in a violent but ultimately unsuccessful coup. In response to street protests and donor pressure, parliament repealed the one-party section of the constitution in December 1991. In 1992, independent Kenya's first multiparty elections were held. Divisions in the opposition contributed to Moi's retention of the presidency in 1992 and again in the 1997 election. Following the 1997 election Kenya experienced its first coalition government as KANU was forced to cobble together a majority by bringing into government a few minor parties.

In October 2002, a coalition of opposition parties formed the National Rainbow Coalition (NARC). In December 2002, the NARC candidate, Mwai Kibaki, was elected the country's third President. President Kibaki received 62% of the vote, and NARC also won 59% of the parliamentary seats. Kibaki, a Kikuyu from Central province, had served as a member of parliament since Kenya's independence in 1963. He served in senior posts in both the Kenyatta and Moi governments, including Vice President and Finance Minister. In 2003, internal conflicts disrupted the NARC government. In 2005 these conflicts came into the open when the government put its draft constitution to a public referendum--key government ministers organized the opposition to the draft constitution, which was defeated soundly. In 2007, two principal leaders of the movement to defeat the draft constitution, Raila Odinga and Kalonzo Musyoka--both former Kibaki allies--were presidential candidates for the Orange Democratic Movement (ODM) party and the Orange Democratic Movement-Kenya (ODM-K) party, respectively. In September 2007, President Kibaki and his allies formed the coalition Party of National Unity (PNU). KANU joined the PNU coalition, although it was serving in parliament as the official opposition party.

On December 27, 2007, Kenya held presidential, parliamentary, and local government elections. While the parliamentary and local government elections were largely credible, the presidential election was seriously flawed, with irregularities in the vote tabulation process as well as turnout in excess of 100% in some constituencies. On December 30, the chairman of the Electoral

Commission of Kenya declared incumbent Mwai Kibaki the winner of the presidential election. Violence erupted in different parts of Kenya as supporters of opposition candidate Raila Odinga and supporters of Kibaki clashed with police and each other. The post-election crisis left about 1,300 Kenyans dead and about 500,000 people displaced. In order to resolve the crisis, negotiation teams representing PNU and ODM began talks under the auspices of former UN Secretary General Kofi Annan and the Panel of Eminent African Persons (Benjamin Mkapa of Tanzania and Graca Machel of Mozambique).

On February 28, 2008, President Kibaki and Raila Odinga signed a power-sharing agreement, which provided for the establishment of a prime minister position (to be filled by Odinga) and two deputy prime minister positions, as well as the division of an expanded list of cabinet posts according to the parties' proportional representation in parliament. On March 18, 2008, the Kenyan parliament amended the constitution and adopted legislation to give legal force to the agreement. On April 17, 2008 the new coalition cabinet and Prime Minister Odinga were sworn in. The Kofi Annan-led political settlement also set out a reform agenda to address underlying causes of the post-election violence. The focus is on constitutional, electoral, land, and institutional reform as well as increased accountability for corruption and political violence. The new constitution was approved in a referendum on August 4, 2010.

Government

The unicameral National Assembly consists of 210 members elected to a term of 5 years from single-member constituencies, plus 12 members nominated by political parties on a proportional representation basis. The president appoints the vice president; under the power-sharing agreement, the president with the agreement of the prime minister makes the initial appointment of cabinet members from among those elected to the assembly. Subsequent cabinet appointments are made by the president in consultation with the prime minister, in accord with the power-sharing agreement's proportional division of cabinet positions. The attorney general and the speaker are ex-officio members of the National Assembly.

The judiciary consists of a Supreme Court, Court of Appeal, High Court, and Magistrates' Courts. The Chief Justice is the highest-ranking judicial official. The Supreme Court was established pursuant to the new constitution.

Local administration is divided among 140 rural districts, each headed by a commissioner appointed by the president. The districts are joined to form seven rural provinces. Nairobi has special provincial status. The Ministry of State in charge of Provincial Administration and Internal Security supervises the administration of districts and provinces.

Once implemented, the new constitution will result in significant changes to this structure, including greater devolution of power to 47 counties and creation of a second legislative chamber with responsibility for representing the interests of the counties and regions. Implementation of the new constitution will take several years, but these key changes in the structure of government should be in place in advance of national elections expected to be held in the second half of 2012.

Principal Government Officials

President--Mwai Kibaki
Vice President--Kalonzo Musyoka
Prime Minister--Raila Odinga
Minister of Foreign Affairs--Moses Wetangula
Ambassador to the United States--Elkanah Odembo
Permanent Representative to the United Nations--Marcharia Kamau
Consulate General Los Angeles--Wenwa Akinyi Odinga Oranga

Kenya maintains an embassy in the United States at 2249 R Street NW, Washington, DC 20008 (tel. 202-387-6101, website: http://www. kenyaembassy.com) and consulates in Los Angeles and New York.

POLITICAL CONDITIONS

Until post-election political unrest struck in early 2008, Kenya had, since independence, maintained considerable stability despite changes in its political system and crises in neighboring countries. This had been particularly true since the re-emergence of multiparty democracy and the accompanying increase in freedom (including freedom of speech, the press, and assembly).

In December 2002, Kenyans held democratic and open elections, which were judged free and fair by international observers. The 2002 elections marked an important turning point in Kenya's democratic evolution as the presidency and the parliamentary majority passed from the party that had ruled Kenya since independence to a coalition of new political parties. The government lost a referendum over its draft constitution in November 2005. This vote too was widely accepted as free, fair, and credible.

Under the first presidency of Mwai Kibaki, the NARC coalition promised to focus its efforts on generating economic growth, improving and expanding education, combating corruption, and rewriting the constitution. The first two goals were largely met, but progress toward the second two goals was limited. President Kibaki's cabinet from 2002-2005 consisted of members of parliament from allied parties and others recruited from opposition parties who joined the cabinet without the approval of their party leaderships.

In early 2006, revelations from investigative reports of two major government-linked corruption scandals rocked Kenya and led to resignations, including three ministers (one of whom was later reappointed). In March 2006, another major scandal was uncovered involving money laundering and tax evasion in the Kenyan banking system. The government's March 2006 raid on the Standard Group media house conducted by masked Kenyan police was internationally condemned and was met with outrage by Kenya media and civil society. The government did not provide a sufficient explanation. No one has been held accountable.

The December 2007 elections were marred by serious irregularities, and set off a wave of violence throughout Kenya. Following the February 2008 signing of a power-sharing agreement between President Kibaki and the opposition, a new coalition cabinet was sworn in April 2008, headed by Prime Minister Odinga. The 42-member cabinet became the largest in Kenya's history, including new ministries for cooperative development, Northern Kenya development, and Nairobi metropolitan development. Several ministries were also subdivided, creating a number of new cabinet positions.

Constitutional reform that addresses the structure of government to create a more effective system of checks and balances is a key element of the reform agenda agreed as part of the power-sharing agreement. Following the process for producing a new draft constitution that was set out in the December 2008 Constitutional Review Act, Kenyans went to the polls on August 4, 2010 to vote on the new constitution. Reflecting broad support for fundamental change, 66.9% of those who voted endorsed it. The new constitution retains Kenya's presidential system but introduces additional checks and balances on executive power and greater devolution of power to the sub-national level. Implementing the new constitution will require passage of several dozen pieces of legislation over a 5-year period.

The International Criminal Court has summoned six Kenyans (five high-ranking government officials and one radio executive) to The Hague on charges of crimes against humanity for their alleged roles in the 2007-2008 post-election violence. They appeared at The Hague in April 2011 to be informed of the charges. Confirmation of charges hearings are being held in September 2011, after which the court will make a decision on whether to proceed to trial.

Economy

Kenya is the largest economy in east Africa and is a regional financial and transportation hub. After independence, Kenya promoted rapid economic growth through public investment, encouragement of smallholder agricultural production, and incentives for private (often foreign) industrial investment. Gross domestic product (GDP) grew at an annual average of 6.6% from 1963 to 1973. Agricultural production grew by 4.7% annually during the same period, stimulated by redistributing estates, diffusing new crop strains, and opening new areas to cultivation.

After experiencing moderately high growth rates during the 1960s and 1970s, Kenya's economic performance during the 1980s and 1990s was far below its potential. From 1991 to 1993, Kenya had its worst economic performance since independence. Growth in GDP stagnated, and agricultural production shrank at an annual rate of 3.9%. Inflation reached a record 100% in August 1993. In the mid-1990s, the government implemented economic reform measures to stabilize the economy and restore sustainable growth, including lifting nearly all administrative controls on producer and retail prices, imports, foreign exchange, and grain marketing. Nevertheless, the economy grew by an annual average of only 1.5% between 1997 and 2002, which was below the population growth estimated at 2.5% per annum, leading to a decline in per capita incomes. The poor economic performance was largely due to inappropriate agricultural, land, and industrial policies compounded by poor international terms of trade and governance weaknesses. Increased government intrusion into the private sector and import substitution policies made the manufacturing sector uncompetitive. The policy environment, along with tight import controls and foreign exchange controls, made the domestic environment for investment unattractive for both foreign and domestic investors.

The Kenyan Government's failure to meet commitments related to governance led to a stop-start relationship with the International Monetary Fund (IMF) and World Bank, both of which suspended support in 1997 and again in 2001.

During President Kibaki's first term in office (2003-2007), the Government of Kenya began an ambitious economic reform program and resumed its cooperation with the World Bank and the IMF. There was some movement to reduce corruption in 2003, but the government did not sustain that momentum. Economic growth began to recover in this period, with real GDP growth registering 2.8% in 2003, 4.3% in 2004, 5.8% in 2005, 6.1% in 2006, and 7.0% in 2007. However, the economic effects of the violence that broke out after the December 27, 2007 general election, compounded by drought and the global financial crisis, brought growth down to less than 2% in 2008. In 2009, there was modest improvement with 2.6% growth, while the final 2010 growth figure was expected to be about 5%.

In May 2009, the IMF Board approved a disbursement of approximately $200 million under its Exogenous Shock Facility (ESF), which is designed to provide policy support and financial assistance to low-income countries facing exogenous but temporary shocks. The ESF resources were meant to help Kenya recover from the negative impact of higher food and international fuel and fertilizer costs, and the slowdown in external demand associated with the global financial crisis. In January 2011, the IMF approved a 3-year, $508.7-million arrangement for Kenya under the Fund's Extended Credit Facility.

To a considerable extent, the government's ability to stimulate economic demand through fiscal and monetary policy is linked to the pace at which the government is pursuing reforms in other key areas. The Privatization Law was enacted in 2005, but only became operational as of January 1, 2008. Parastatals Kenya Electricity Generating Company (KenGen), Telkom Kenya, and Kenya Re-Insurance have been privatized. The government sold 25% of Safaricom (10 billion shares) in 2008, reducing its share to 35%. Accelerating growth to achieve Kenya's potential and reduce the poverty that afflicts about 46% of its population will require continued deregulation of business, improved delivery of government services, addressing structural reforms, massive investment in new infrastructure (especially roads), reduction of chronic insecurity caused by crime, and improved economic governance generally. The government's Vision 2030 plan calls for these reforms, but realization of the goals could be delayed by coalition politics and line ministries' limited capacity.

Economic expansion is fairly broad-based and is built on a stable macro-environment fostered by government, and the resilience, resourcefulness, and improved confidence of the private sector. Despite the post-election crisis, Nairobi continues to be the primary communication and financial hub of East Africa. It enjoys the region's best transportation linkages, communications infrastructure, and trained personnel, although these advantages are less prominent than in past years.

In FY 2010, tea was Kenya's top export, accounting for $1.15 billion. Fresh horticulture exports were $718 million, well short of the record high of $1.12 billion in 2007, in part due to unfavorable global weather conditions that affected air transportation. Tourism has rebounded from the drop experienced in 2008 after the post-election violence, bringing in $807 million in 2009, an increase of 19% from 2008. In 2010, the Kenyan Ministry of Tourism recorded nearly 1.1 million tourists--an all-time high--and an 18% revenue growth, in local currency terms. Africa is Kenya's largest export market, followed by the European Union (EU). Kenya benefits significantly from the African Growth and Opportunity Act (AGOA), but the apparel industry is struggling to hold its ground against Asian competition. Currently there are 19 apparel factories, 1 yarn/fabric company, and 6 accessory companies (labels, sewing supplies, hangers) operating in the Export Processing Zones. Approximately 90% of Kenya's AGOA exports in 2010 were garments, and Kenya's garment exports under AGOA totaled $202 million in 2010 (a slight increase over 2009 but still well below the 2006 level of $265 million).

Kenya does not systematically collect foreign direct investment (FDI) statistics, and its historical performance in attracting FDI has been relatively weak. The stock of FDI in 2005 was estimated to be about $1.04 billion, less than half of that in neighboring Tanzania. Net foreign direct investment was negative from 2000-2003, but started trickling back in 2004. The stock of U.S. FDI (at historical prices) was estimated to be about U.S. $180 million as of 2010.

Remittances are Kenya's single largest source of foreign exchange and a key social safety net. According to the Central Bank of Kenya, recorded remittances totaled about $640 million in 2010; however, the actual number may be as high as $1 billion.

Kenya faces profound environmental challenges brought on by high population growth, deforestation, shifting climate patterns, and the overgrazing of cattle in marginal areas in the north and west of the country. Significant portions of the population will continue to require emergency food assistance in the coming years.

Kenya is pursuing regional economic integration, which could enhance long-term growth prospects. The government is pursuing a strategy to reduce unemployment by expanding its manufacturing base to export more value-added goods to the region while enabling Kenya to develop its services hub. In March 1996, the Presidents of Kenya, Tanzania, and Uganda re-established the East African Community (EAC). The EAC's objectives include harmonizing tariffs and customs regimes, free movement of people, and improving regional infrastructures. In March 2004, the three East African countries signed a Customs Union Agreement paving the way for a common market. The Customs Union and a Common External Tariff were established on January 1, 2005, but the EAC countries are still working out exceptions to the tariff. Rwanda and Burundi joined the community in July 2007. In May 2007, during a Common Market for Eastern and Southern Africa (COMESA) summit, 13 heads of state endorsed a move to adopt a COMESA customs union and set December 8, 2008 as the target date for its adoption. On July 1, 2010, the EAC Common Market Protocol, which allows for the free movement of goods and services across the five member states, took effect. In October 2008, the heads of state of EAC, COMESA, and the Southern African Development Community (SADC) agreed to work toward a free trade area among all three economic groups with the eventual goal of establishing a customs union. If realized, the Tripartite Free Trade area would cover 26 countries.

Media

The key independent print media in Kenya are the Nation Media Group, the Standard Group, People Limited, and the Times Media Group. The Nation Media Group publications, which include the Daily Nation, the Sunday Nation, the Business Daily, the weekly East African, and the only Swahili publications, Taifa Leo and Taifa Jumapili, have the largest circulations. The Standard and the Sunday Standard, published by the Standard Group, are also popular newspapers, although with smaller circulations. Approximately 120 foreign correspondents representing 100 media organizations report from Nairobi. There is no government-owned or controlled newspaper.

Major independent radio and television media are the Kenya Television Network (KTN), the broadcast media arm of the Standard Group; Nation Radio/TV, owned by the Nation Media Group; and Citizen Radio/Television, owned by Royal Media Services. The government owns and controls the

Kenya Broadcasting Corporation (KBC) and its subsidiaries. KBC is the only national radio and television network.

Kenya also has hundreds of FM radio stations, some broadcasting in Swahili or in local languages. Radio has a wide reach in Kenya, especially in rural areas. Some major international broadcasters, including British Broadcasting Corporation (BBC), Voice of America (VOA), and Radio France Internationale (RFI), rebroadcast their programming in Kenya.

FOREIGN RELATIONS

Despite internal tensions in Sudan and Ethiopia, Kenya has maintained good relations with them. Relations with Uganda and Tanzania are strengthening as the three countries work for mutual economic benefit.

Kenya has hosted and played an active role in the negotiations to resolve the civil war in Sudan and to reinstate a central government authority in Somalia. On January 9, 2005 a Sudan North-South Comprehensive Peace Accord was signed in Nairobi. In July 2011 South Sudan became an independent state. Negotiations in the Somali National Reconciliation Conference resulted at the end of 2004 in the establishment of Somali Transitional Federal Institutions (Assembly, President, Prime Minister, and Government). Until early 2005, Kenya served as a major host for these institutions. Between May and June 2005, members of the Somalia Transitional Federal Institutions relocated to Somalia. Kenya is host to more than 550,000 refugees, most of whom are from Somalia.

Kenya's relations with Western countries are generally friendly, although current political and economic instabilities are sometimes blamed on Western pressures.

U.S.-KENYAN RELATIONS

The United States and Kenya have enjoyed cordial relations since Kenya's independence. Relations became even closer after Kenya's democratic transition of 2002 and subsequent improvements in civil liberties.

Approximately 15,000 U.S. citizens are registered with the U.S. Embassy as residents of Kenya. More than 100,000 Americans visited Kenya in 2010. About two-thirds of resident Americans are missionaries and their families.

U.S. business investment primarily is in commerce, light manufacturing, and the tourism industry.

Al Qaeda terrorists bombed the U.S. Embassy in Nairobi on August 7, 1998, taking hundreds of lives and maiming thousands more. Since that event, the Kenyan and U.S. Governments have intensified cooperation to address all forms of insecurity in Kenya, including terrorism. The United States provides equipment and training to Kenyan security forces, both civilian and military. In its dialogue with the Kenyan Government, the United States urges effective action against corruption and insecurity as the two greatest impediments to Kenya achieving sustained, rapid economic growth.

U.S. assistance to Kenya is substantial. It promotes broad-based economic development as the basis for continued progress in political, social, and related areas of national life. The U.S. assistance strategy is built around five broad objectives: advancing shared democratic values, human rights, and good governance; fighting disease and improving healthcare; fighting poverty and promoting private sector-led prosperity; cooperating to fight insecurity and terrorism; and collaborating to foster peace and stability in East Africa. The Peace Corps, which usually has about 150 volunteers in Kenya, is integral to the overall U.S. assistance strategy in Kenya.

In: Humanitarian Crisis and Response ...   ISBN: 978-1-61942-540-8
Editors: C.J. Newsome and H.I. Herron © 2012 Nova Science Publishers, Inc.

Chapter 11

ETHIOPIA COUNTRY PROFILE

United States Department of State

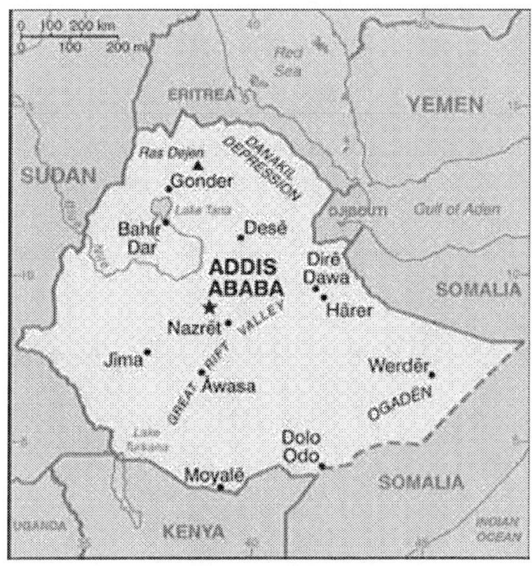

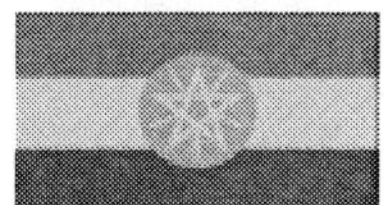

Flag of Ethiopia.

GEOGRAPHY

Area: 1.1 million sq. km (472,000 sq. mi.); about the size of Texas, Oklahoma, and New Mexico combined.

Cities: *Capital*--Addis Ababa (pop. 3 million, 2010 est.). *Other cities--* Dire Dawa (379,896), Nazret (189,000), Gondar (229,368), Dessie (133.007), Mekelle (238,852), Bahir Dar (199,568), Jimma (132,000), Awassa (176,267).

Terrain: High plateau, mountains, dry lowland plains.

Climate: Temperate in the highlands; hot in the lowlands.

PEOPLE

Nationality: *Noun and adjective*--Ethiopian(s).

Population (est.): 82 million.

Annual population growth rate (est.): 2.6%.

Ethnic groups (est.): Oromo 34.5%, Amhara 26.9%, Tigre 6.1%, Somali 6.2%, Sidama 4%, Gurage 2.5%, Wolaita 2.3%, Afar 1.7%, other nationalities 3%.

Religions (est.): Ethiopian Orthodox Christian 43.5%, Muslim 33.9%, Protestant 18.6%, remainder indigenous beliefs.

Languages: Amharic (official), Tigrinya, Arabic, Guaragigna, Oromifa, English, Somali.

Education: *Years compulsory*--none. *Attendance* (elementary)--87.9%. *Literacy*--43%.

Health: *Infant mortality rate*--77/1,000 live births.

Work force: *Agriculture*--80%. *Industry and commerce*--20%.

GOVERNMENT

Type: Federal republic.

Constitution: Ratified 1994.

Branches: *Executive*--president, Council of State, Council of Ministers. Executive power resides with the prime minister. *Legislative*--bicameral parliament. *Judicial*--divided into federal and regional courts.

Administrative subdivisions: 9 regions and 2 special city administrations: Addis Ababa and Dire Dawa.

Political parties: Ethiopian People's Revolutionary Democratic Front (EPRDF), the Unity for Democracy and Justice (UDJ) party, the United Ethiopian Democratic Forces (UEDF), Oromo Federalist Democratic Movement (OFDM), and other small parties.

Suffrage: Universal starting at age 18.

Central government budget (2009-2010): $6.0 billion.

Defense: $341 million (1.14% of GDP FY 2009-2010).

National holiday: May 28.

ECONOMY

GDP (FY 2009-2010): $29.9 billion.

Annual growth rate (2009-2010): 10.4%.

GDP per capita (2009-2010): $365.

Average inflation rate (FY 2009-2010): 2.8%.

Natural resources: Potash, salt, gold, copper, platinum, natural gas (unexploited).

Agriculture (42% of GDP): *Products*--coffee, cereals, pulses, oilseeds, khat, meat, hides and skins. *Cultivated land--17%.*

Industry (13% of GDP): *Types*--textiles, processed foods, construction, cement, and hydroelectric power.

Services (45% of GDP).

Trade (2009-2010): *Exports*--$2.0 billion. *Imports*--$8.4 billion; plus remittances--official est. $2 billion.

Fiscal year: July 8-July 7.

Geography

Ethiopia is located in the Horn of Africa and is bordered on the north and northeast by Eritrea, on the east by Djibouti and Somalia, on the south by Kenya, and on the west and southwest by Sudan. The country has a high central plateau that varies from 1,800 to 3,000 meters (6,000 ft.-10,000 ft.) above sea level, with some mountains reaching 4,620 meters (15,158 ft.). Elevation is generally highest just before the point of descent to the Great Rift Valley, which splits the plateau diagonally. A number of rivers cross the plateau--notably the Blue Nile flowing from Lake Tana. The plateau gradually slopes to the lowlands of the Sudan on the west and the Somali-inhabited plains to the southeast.

The climate is temperate on the plateau and hot in the lowlands. At Addis Ababa, which ranges from 2,200 to 2,600 meters (7,000 ft.-8,500 ft.), maximum temperature is 26° C (80° F) and minimum 4° C (40° F). The weather is usually sunny and dry with the short (belg) rains occurring February-April and the big (meher) rains beginning in mid-June and ending in mid-September.

People

Ethiopia's population is highly diverse. Most of its people speak a Semitic or Cushitic language. The Oromo, Amhara, and Tigreans make up more than two-thirds of the population, but there are more than 77 different ethnic groups with their own distinct languages within Ethiopia. Some of these have as few as 10,000 members. In general, most of the Christians live in the highlands, while Muslims and adherents of traditional African religions tend to inhabit lowland regions. English is the most widely spoken foreign language and is taught in all secondary schools. Amharic is the official language and was the language of primary school instruction but has been replaced in many areas by local languages such as Oromifa and Tigrinya.

History

Hominid bones discovered in eastern Ethiopia dating back 4.4 million years make Ethiopia one of the earliest known locations of human ancestors. Ethiopia is the oldest independent country in Africa and one of the oldest in the world. Herodotus, the Greek historian of the fifth century B.C., describes ancient Ethiopia in his writings. The Old Testament of the Bible records the Queen of Sheba's visit to Jerusalem. According to legend, Menelik I, the son of King Solomon and the Queen of Sheba, founded the Ethiopian Empire. Missionaries from Egypt and Syria introduced Christianity in the fourth century A.D. Following the rise of Islam in the seventh century, Ethiopia was gradually cut off from European Christendom. The Portuguese established contact with Ethiopia in 1493, primarily to strengthen their influence over the Indian Ocean and to convert Ethiopia to Roman Catholicism. There followed a century of conflict between pro- and anti-Catholic factions, resulting in the expulsion of all foreign missionaries in the 1630s. This period of bitter religious conflict contributed to hostility toward foreign Christians and Europeans, which persisted into the 20th century and was a factor in Ethiopia's isolation until the mid-19th century.

Under the Emperors Theodore II (1855-68), Johannes IV (1872-89), and Menelik II (1889-1913), the kingdom was consolidated and began to emerge from its medieval isolation. When Menelik II died, his grandson, Lij Iyassu, succeeded to the throne but soon lost support because of his Muslim ties. The Christian nobility deposed him in 1916, and Menelik's daughter, Zewditu, was made empress. Her cousin, Ras Tafari Makonnen (1892-1975), was made regent and successor to the throne. In 1930, after the empress died, the regent, adopting the throne name Haile Selassie, was crowned emperor. His reign was interrupted in 1936 when Italian Fascist forces invaded and occupied Ethiopia. The emperor was forced into exile in England. Five years later, British and Ethiopian forces defeated the Italians, and the emperor returned to the throne.

Following civil unrest, which began in February 1974, the aging Haile Selassie I was deposed on September 12, 1974 by a provisional administrative council of soldiers, known as the Derg ("committee"). The Derg seized power, installing a government that was socialist in name and military in style. It then summarily executed 59 members of the royal family and ministers and generals of the emperor's government; Emperor Haile Selassie I was strangled in the basement of his palace on August 22, 1975.

The Derg's collapse was hastened by droughts, famine, and insurrections, particularly in the northern regions of Tigray and Eritrea. In 1989, the Tigrayan People's Liberation Front (TPLF) merged with other ethnically based opposition movements to form the Ethiopian Peoples' Revolutionary Democratic Front (EPRDF). In May 1991, EPRDF forces advanced on Addis Ababa. Mengistu fled the country for asylum in Zimbabwe, where he still resides.

In July 1991, the EPRDF, the Oromo Liberation Front (OLF), and others established the Transitional Government of Ethiopia (TGE) comprised of an 87-member Council of Representatives and guided by a national charter that functioned as a transitional constitution. In June 1992 the OLF withdrew from the government; in March 1993, members of the Southern Ethiopia Peoples' Democratic Coalition left the government.

In May 1991, the Eritrean People's Liberation Front (EPLF), led by Isaias Afwerki, assumed control of Eritrea and established a provisional government. This provisional government independently administered Eritrea until April 23-25, 1993, when Eritreans voted overwhelmingly for independence in a UN-monitored free and fair referendum. Eritrea, with Ethiopia's consent, was declared independent on April 27. The United States recognized its independence the next day.

In Ethiopia, President Meles Zenawi and members of the TGE pledged to oversee the formation of a multi-party democracy. The election for a 547-member constituent assembly was held in June 1994. The assembly adopted the constitution of the Federal Democratic Republic of Ethiopia in December 1994. The elections for Ethiopia's first popularly chosen national parliament and regional legislatures were held in May and June 1995. Most opposition parties chose to boycott these elections, ensuring a landslide victory for the EPRDF. International and non-governmental observers concluded that opposition parties would have been able to participate had they chosen to do so. The Government of the Federal Democratic Republic of Ethiopia was installed in August 1995.

In May 1998, Eritrean forces attacked part of the Ethiopia-Eritrea border region, seizing some Ethiopian-controlled territory. The strike spurred a 2-year war between the neighboring states that cost over 70,000 lives. On June 18, 2000, Ethiopian and Eritrean leaders signed an Agreement on Cessation of Hostilities and on December 12, 2000, a peace agreement, known as the Algiers Agreement.

Opposition candidates won 12 seats in national parliamentary elections in 2000. In controversial national elections in May 2005, the opposition was awarded 170 of 547 seats but claimed fraud; violence ensued. Ethiopian security forces responded and in the process killed over 200 people, arrested scores of opposition leaders, as well as journalists and human rights advocates, and detained tens of thousands of civilians for up to 3 months in rural detention camps. In December 2005, the government charged 131 opposition, media, and civil society leaders with capital offenses including "outrages against the constitution." Key opposition leaders and almost all of the 131 were pardoned and released from prison 18 months later. The opposition largely boycotted local elections in 2008 with the result that EPRDF won more than 99% of all local seats.

In June 2008, former CUD vice-chairman Birtukan Mideksa was elected the party chairman of the new Unity for Democracy and Justice (UDJ) party at its inaugural session in Addis Ababa. In October 2008 the Ethiopian Government arrested over 100 Oromo leaders, accusing some of being members of the outlawed Oromo Liberation Front (OLF). At the end of December 2008, after detaining Birtukan several times briefly during the month, the government re-arrested her, saying that she had violated the conditions of her pardon (she was one of the prominent opposition leaders pardoned by the government in the summer of 2007). Her original sentence of life imprisonment was reinstated and she remained in prison until she was pardoned and released on October 6, 2010.

In April 2009 the Ethiopian Government arrested 40 individuals, mostly Amhara military or ex-military members allegedly affiliated with Ginbot 7, an external opposition party, for their suspected involvement in a terrorist assassination plot of government leaders. This party was founded in May 2008 in the United States by Berhanu Nega, one of the opposition leaders in the 2005 elections, and advocates for change in the government "by any means." In August 2009, the Federal High Court found 13 of the defendants guilty in absentia and one not guilty in absentia. In November 2009, the court found another 27 guilty.

In simultaneous national and regional parliamentary elections in May 2010, the ruling EPRDF won more than 99% of all legislative seats in the country. In a tally of the popular vote, 91.95% voted for EPRDF and affiliate parties, while only 8.05% voted for the opposition countrywide. Election Day was peaceful as 89% of registered voters cast ballots, but independent observation of the vote was severely limited. Only European Union and African Union observers were permitted, and they were restricted to the capital and barred from proximity to polling places. Although those few independent observers allowed access to the process did not question the EPRDF victory, there was ample evidence that unsavory government tactics--including intimidation of opposition candidates and supporters--influenced the extent of the victory.

Overall, the 2010 elections were not up to international standards because the environment conducive to free and fair elections was not in place. The EPRDF used the advantages of incumbency to restrict political space for opposition candidates and activists. At the local level, thousands of opposition activists complained of EPRDF-sponsored mistreatment ranging from harassment in submitting candidacy forms to beatings by local militia members, and complained further that there was no non-EPRDF dominated forum to which to present those complaints.

GOVERNMENT AND POLITICAL CONDITIONS

Ethiopia is a federal republic under the 1994 constitution. The executive branch includes a president, Council of State, and Council of Ministers.

Executive power resides with the prime minister. There is a bicameral parliament; national legislative elections were held in 2010. The judicial branch comprises federal and regional courts. Following the 2010 elections, there were 152 women in the 547-seat parliament, two female judges on the 11-seat Supreme Court, and three women among the 39 state ministers.

Political parties include the Ethiopian People's Revolutionary Democratic Front (EPRDF), Unity for Democracy and Justice (UDJ), Oromo People's Congress (OPC), Arena Tigay for Democracy and Sovereignty, Oromo Federalist Democratic Movement (OFDM), Coalition for Unity and Democracy Party (CUDP), the United Ethiopian Democratic Forces (UEDF), All Ethiopia Unity Party (AEUP), and other small parties. Suffrage is universal at age 18.

The EPRDF-led government of Prime Minister Meles Zenawi has promoted a policy of ethnic federalism, devolving significant powers to regional, ethnically based authorities. Ethiopia has nine semi-autonomous administrative regions and two special city administrations (Addis Ababa and Dire Dawa), which have the power to raise their own revenues.

Principal Government Officials

President--Girma Wolde-Giorgis
Prime Minister--Meles Zenawi
Deputy Prime Minister and Minister of Foreign Affairs--Hailemariam Desalegn
Minister of National Defense--Siraj Fegisa
Mayor of Addis Ababa--Kuma Demeska
Ambassador to the U.S.--Girma Birru
Ethiopia maintains an embassy in the U.S. at 3506 International Drive, NW, Washington, DC 20008 (tel. 202-364-1200). It also maintains a UN mission in New York and consulates in Los Angeles, Seattle (honorary), and Houston (honorary).

Economy

The current government has embarked on a cautious program of economic reform, including privatization of state enterprises and rationalization of government regulation. While the process is still ongoing, so far the reforms have attracted only meager foreign investment, and the government remains heavily involved in the economy.

The Ethiopian economy is based on agriculture, which contributes 42% to GDP and more than 80% of exports, and employs 80% of the population. The major agricultural export crop is coffee, providing approximately 26% of Ethiopia's foreign exchange earnings, down from 65% a decade ago because of the slump in coffee prices since the mid-1990s and increases in other exports. Other traditional major agricultural exports are leather, hides and skins, pulses, oilseeds, and the traditional "khat," a leafy narcotic that is chewed. Sugar and gold production has also become important in recent years.

Ethiopia's agriculture is plagued by periodic drought, soil degradation caused by inappropriate agricultural practices and overgrazing, deforestation, high population density, undeveloped water resources, and poor transport infrastructure, making it difficult and expensive to get goods to market. Yet agriculture is the country's most promising resource. Potential exists for self-sufficiency in grains and for export development in livestock, flowers, grains, oilseeds, sugar, vegetables, and fruits.

Gold, marble, limestone, and small amounts of tantalum are mined in Ethiopia. Other resources with potential for commercial development include large potash deposits, natural gas, iron ore, and possibly oil and geothermal energy. Although Ethiopia has good hydroelectric resources, which power most of its manufacturing sector, it is totally dependent on imports for oil. A landlocked country, Ethiopia has relied on the port of Djibouti since the 1998-2000 border war with Eritrea. Ethiopia is connected with the port of Djibouti by road. Of the 49,000 kilometers of all-weather roads in Ethiopia, 15% are asphalt. Mountainous terrain and the lack of good roads and sufficient vehicles make land transportation difficult and expensive. Ethiopian Airlines serves 17 domestic airfields and has 60 international destinations.

Dependent on a few vulnerable crops for its foreign exchange earnings and reliant on imported oil, Ethiopia is suffering a severe lack of foreign exchange. The largely subsistence economy is incapable of meeting the budget requirements for drought relief, an ambitious development plan, and indispensable imports such as oil. The gap has largely been covered through foreign assistance inflows.

DEFENSE

The Ethiopian National Defense Forces (ENDF) numbers about 200,000 personnel, which makes it one of the largest militaries in Africa. During the 1998-2000 border war with Eritrea, the ENDF mobilized strength reached approximately 350,000. Since the end of the war, some 150,000 soldiers have been demobilized. With the aid of the U.S. and other countries, the ENDF continues a transition from its roots as a guerrilla army to an all-volunteer professional military organization. Training in peacekeeping operations, professional military education, military training management, counterterrorism operations, and military medicine are among the major programs sponsored by the United States. Ethiopia has one peacekeeping contingent in Liberia. In January 2009, Ethiopian peacekeeping troops had begun deploying in Darfur. As of September 2010, the Ethiopian contingent there consisted of 2,366 troops and five attack helicopters.

FOREIGN RELATIONS

Ethiopia was relatively isolated from major movements of world politics until Italian invasions in 1895 and 1935. Since World War II, Ethiopia has played an active role in world and African affairs. Ethiopia was a charter member of the United Nations and took part in UN operations in Korea in 1951 and the Congo in 1960. Former Emperor Haile Selassie was a founder of the Organization of African Unity (OAU), now known as the African Union (AU). Addis Ababa also hosts the UN Economic Commission for Africa. Ethiopia is also a member of the Intergovernmental Authority on Development (IGAD), a Horn of Africa regional grouping.

Although nominally a member of the Non-Aligned Movement, after the 1974 revolution, Ethiopia moved into a close relationship with the Soviet Union and its allies and supported their international policies and positions until the change of government in 1991. Today, Ethiopia has good relations with the United States and the West, especially in responding to regional instability and supporting counterterrorism efforts.

Ethiopia's relations with Eritrea have remained tense and unresolved following the brutal 1998-2000 border war. The two countries signed a peace agreement in December 2000. A five-member independent international commission--the Eritrea Ethiopia Boundary Commission (EEBC)--issued a decision in April 2002 delimiting the border. In November 2007 the EEBC issued a decision that the border was demarcated based on map coordinates (usual demarcation based on pillars on the ground had not yet occurred due to disagreement between Ethiopia and Eritrea) and disbanded. Ethiopia does not consider the border to be demarcated, though Eritrea does. In July 2008 the United Nations Mission in Ethiopia and Eritrea (UNMEE) peacekeeping mission was terminated due to Eritrean restrictions impeding UNMEE's ability to operate. Both countries have stationed approximately 100,000 troops along the border. Both countries insist they will not instigate fighting, but both also remain prepared for any eventuality.

The irredentist claims of the extremist-controlled Council of Islamic Courts (CIC) in Somalia in 2006 posed a security threat to Ethiopia and to the Transitional Federal Government (TFG) of Somalia. In December 2006, the TFG requested the assistance of the Ethiopian military to respond to the CIC's growing strength within Somalia. Within a few weeks, the joint Ethiopian-TFG forces routed the CIC from Somalia. Subsequently, Ethiopia stationed troops in Somalia (largely around Mogadishu), awaiting full deployment of the African Union's Mission in Somalia (AMISOM). However, the slow buildup of AMISOM troop levels pushed the Ethiopian Government to announce that its army would withdraw from the country in a matter of weeks. By the end of January 2009, all of its 3,000-4,000 troops had left the country. While Ethiopia does not currently have a military presence in Somalia, it views the ongoing conflict as a key national security concern.

U.S.-ETHIOPIA RELATIONS

U.S.-Ethiopian relations were established in 1903 and were good throughout the period prior to the Italian occupation in 1935. After World War II, these ties strengthened on the basis of a September 1951 treaty of amity and economic relations. In 1953, two agreements were signed: a mutual defense assistance agreement, under which the United States agreed to furnish military equipment and training, and an accord regularizing the operations of a U.S. communication facility at Asmara. Through fiscal year 1978, the United States provided Ethiopia with $282 million in military assistance and $366 million in economic assistance in agriculture, education, public health, and transportation. A Peace Corps program emphasized education, and U.S. Information Service educational and cultural exchanges were numerous.

After Ethiopia's revolution, the bilateral relationship began to cool due to the Derg's linkage with international communism and U.S. revulsion at the Derg's human rights abuses. The United States rebuffed Ethiopia's request for increased military assistance to intensify its fight against the Eritrean secessionist movement and to repel the Somali invasion. In July 1980, the U.S. Ambassador to Ethiopia was recalled at the request of the Ethiopian Government, and the U.S. Embassy in Ethiopia and the Ethiopian Embassy in the United States were headed by Charges d'Affaires. The International Security and Development Act of 1985 prohibited all U.S. economic assistance to Ethiopia with the exception of humanitarian disaster and emergency relief.

With the downfall of the Mengistu regime, U.S.-Ethiopian relations improved dramatically. Legislative restrictions on assistance to Ethiopia other than humanitarian assistance were lifted. Diplomatic relations were upgraded to the ambassadorial level in 1992. Total U.S. Government assistance, including food aid, between 1999 and 2009 was $4.7 billion. The U.S. Government provided $862 million in assistance in FY 2009, $345 million of it for combating HIV/AIDS. In addition, the U.S. Government donated more than $374 million in food assistance in 2009 to help the government cope with a severe drought.

Today, Ethiopia is an important regional security partner of the United States. U.S. development assistance to Ethiopia is focused on reducing famine vulnerability, hunger, and poverty and emphasizes economic, governance, and social sector policy reforms. Some military training funds, including training in such issues as the laws of war and observance of human rights, also are provided but are explicitly limited to non-lethal assistance and training.

In: Humanitarian Crisis and Response ...   ISBN: 978-1-61942-540-8
Editors: C.J. Newsome and H.I. Herron © 2012 Nova Science Publishers, Inc.

Chapter 12

ERITREA COUNTRY PROFILE

United States Department of State

Official Name: State of Eritrea

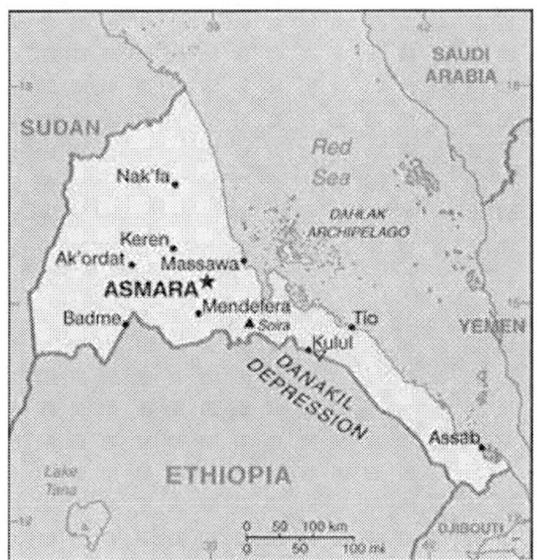

Flag of Eritrea.

GEOGRAPHY

Area: 125,000 sq. km. (48,000 sq. mi.); about the size of Pennsylvania.

Cities: *Capital*--Asmara (est. pop. 435,000). *Other cities*--Keren (57,000); Assab (28,000); Massawa (25,000); Afabet (25,000); Tessenie (25,000); Mendefera (25,000); Dekemhare (20,000); Adekeieh (15,000); Barentu (15,000); Ghinda (15,000).

Terrain: Central highlands straddle escarpment associated with Rift Valley, dry coastal plains, and western lowlands.

Climate: Temperate in the highlands; hot in the lowlands.

PEOPLE

Nationality: *Noun and adjective*--Eritrean(s).

Population (2010 est.): 5.6 million.

Annual population growth rate: 2.5%.

Ethnic groups: Tigrinya 50%, Tigre 31.4%, Saho 5%, Afar 5%, Beja 2.5%, Bilen 2.1%, Kunama 2%, Nara 1.5%, and Rashaida 0.5%.

Religions: Christian 50%, mostly Orthodox, Muslim 48%, indigenous beliefs 2%.

Education: *Years compulsory*--none. *Attendance*--elementary (net 2002) 45.2%; secondary (net 2002) 21.2%.

Health: *Infant mortality rate* (2003)--43/1,000. *Life expectancy*--61 years.

Work force (2009): Agriculture--17.3%; services--59.5%; industry--23.2%.

GOVERNMENT

Type: Transitional government.

Independence: Eritrea officially celebrated its independence on May 24, 1993.

Constitution: Ratified May 24, 1997, but not yet implemented.

Branches: *Executive*--president, cabinet. *Legislative*--Transitional National Assembly (does not meet). *Judicial*--Supreme Court.

Administrative subdivisions: Six administrative regions.

Political party: People's Front for Democracy and Justice (name adopted by the Eritrean People's Liberation Front when it established itself as a political party).

Suffrage: Universal, age 18 and above (although no national elections have been held).

Central government budget (2005 est.): $485 million.

Defense (2004 est.): $185 million.

ECONOMY

Real GDP (2009 est.): $1.87 billion.

Annual growth rate (2009 est.): 3.6%.

Per capita GNI (2008, World Bank): $640 (purchasing power parity); $300 (Atlas method).

Avg. inflation rate (2008 est.): 18%.

Mineral resources: Gold, copper, iron ore, potash, oil.

Agriculture (24% of GDP in 2007): *Products*--millet, sorghum, teff, wheat, barley, flax, cotton, papayas, citrus fruits, bananas, beans and lentils, potatoes, vegetables, fish, dairy products, meat, and skins. *Cultivated land*--10% of arable land.

Industry (19% of GDP in 2007): *Types*--processed food and dairy products, alcoholic beverages, leather goods, textiles, chemicals, cement and other construction materials, salt, paper, and matches.

Trade: *Exports* (2005 est.)--$12 million: skins, meat, live sheep and cattle, gum arabic. *Major markets*--Middle East (Saudi Arabia, Yemen), Europe (Italy), Djibouti, and Sudan. *Imports* (2005 est.)--$474 million: food, military materiel, and fuel, manufactured goods, machinery and transportation equipment. *Major suppliers*--U.A.E., Saudi Arabia, Italy, Germany, Belgium.

Geography

Eritrea is located in the Horn of Africa and is bordered on the northeast and east by the Red Sea, on the west and northwest by Sudan, on the south by Ethiopia, and on the southeast by Djibouti. The country has a high central plateau that varies from 1,800 to 3,000 meters (6,000-10,000 ft.) above sea level. A coastal plain, western lowlands, and some 300 islands comprise the remainder of Eritrea's landmass. Eritrea has no year-round rivers.

The climate is temperate in the mountains and hot in the lowlands. Asmara, the capital, is about 2,300 meters (7,500 ft.) above sea level. Maximum temperature is 26° C (80° F). The weather is usually sunny and dry, with the short or belg rains occurring February-April and the big or meher rains beginning in late June and ending in mid-September.

People

Eritrea's population comprises nine ethnic groups, most of whom speak Semitic or Cushitic languages. The Tigrinya and Tigre make up four-fifths of the population and speak different, but somewhat mutually intelligible, Semitic languages. In general, most of the Christians live in the highlands, while Muslims and adherents of traditional beliefs live in lowland regions. Tigrinya and Arabic are the most frequently used languages for commercial and official transactions. In urban areas, English is widely spoken and is the language used for secondary and university education.

History

Prior to Italian colonization in 1885, what is now Eritrea had been ruled by the various local or international powers that successively dominated the Red Sea region. In 1896, the Italians used Eritrea as a springboard for their disastrous attempt to conquer Ethiopia. Eritrea was placed under British military administration after the Italian surrender in World War II. In 1952, a UN resolution federating Eritrea with Ethiopia went into effect. The resolution ignored Eritrean pleas for independence but guaranteed Eritreans some democratic rights and a measure of autonomy. Almost immediately after the federation went into effect, however, these rights began to be abridged or violated.

In 1962, Emperor Haile Sellassie unilaterally dissolved the Eritrean parliament and annexed the country, sparking the Eritrean fight for independence from Ethiopia that continued after Haile Sellassie was ousted in a coup in 1974. The new Ethiopian Government, known as the Derg, was a Marxist military junta led by Ethiopian strongman Mengistu Haile Miriam.

During the 1960s, the Eritrean Liberation Front (ELF) led the Eritrean independence struggle. In 1970, some members of the group broke away to form the Eritrean People's Liberation Front (EPLF). By the late 1970s, the

EPLF had become the dominant armed Eritrean group fighting against the Ethiopian Government, with Isaias Afwerki as its leader. The EPLF used material captured from the Ethiopian Army to fight against the government.

By 1977, the EPLF was poised to drive the Ethiopians out of Eritrea. That same year, however, a massive airlift of Soviet arms to Ethiopia enabled the Ethiopian Army to regain the initiative and forced the EPLF to retreat to the bush. Between 1978 and 1986, the Derg launched eight major offensives against the independence movement--all of which failed. In 1988, the EPLF captured Afabet, headquarters of the Ethiopian Army in northeastern Eritrea, prompting the Ethiopian Army to withdraw from its garrisons in Eritrea's western lowlands. EPLF fighters then moved into position around Keren, Eritrea's second-largest city. Meanwhile, other dissident movements were making headway throughout Ethiopia. At the end of the 1980s, the Soviet Union informed Mengistu that it would not be renewing the existing bilateral defense and cooperation agreement. With the withdrawal of Soviet support and supplies, the Ethiopian Army's morale plummeted, and the EPLF--along with other Ethiopian rebel forces--advanced on Ethiopian positions.

The United States played a facilitative role in the peace talks in Washington during the months leading up to the May 1991 fall of the Mengistu regime. In mid-May, Mengistu resigned as head of the Ethiopian Government and went into exile in Zimbabwe, leaving a caretaker government in Addis Ababa. Later that month, the United States chaired talks in London to formalize the end of the war. The four major combatant groups, including the EPLF, attended these talks.

Having defeated the Ethiopian forces in Eritrea, EPLF troops took control of their homeland. In May 1991, the EPLF established the Provisional Government of Eritrea (PGE) to administer Eritrean affairs until a referendum could be held on independence and a permanent government established. EPLF leader Isaias became the head of the PGE, and the EPLF Central Committee served as its legislative body.

A high-level U.S. delegation was present in Addis Ababa for the July 1-5, 1991 conference that established a transitional government in Ethiopia. The EPLF attended the July conference as an observer and held talks with the new transitional government regarding Eritrea's relationship to Ethiopia. The outcome of those talks was an agreement in which the Ethiopians recognized the right of the Eritreans to hold a referendum on independence.

Although some EPLF cadres had espoused a Marxist ideology, Soviet assistance for Mengistu limited the level of Eritrean interest in seeking Soviet support. The fall of communist regimes in the former Soviet Union and the

Eastern Bloc convinced the Eritreans it was a failed system. The EPLF (and later its successor, the PFDJ) expressed commitment to establishing a democratic form of government and a free-market economy in Eritrea. The United States agreed to provide assistance to both Ethiopia and Eritrea, conditional on continued progress toward democracy and human rights.

On April 23-25, 1993, Eritreans voted overwhelmingly for independence from Ethiopia in a UN-monitored free and fair referendum. The Eritrean authorities declared Eritrea an independent state on April 27, and Eritrea officially celebrated its independence on May 24, 1993.

GOVERNMENT AND POLITICAL CONDITIONS

Eritrea's Government faced formidable challenges following independence. With no constitution, no judicial system, and an education system in shambles, the Eritrean Government was required to build institutions of government from scratch. Currently, the Government of Eritrea exercises strict control of political, social, and economic systems, with nearly no civil liberties allowed.

On May 19, 1993, the PGE issued a proclamation regarding the reorganization of the government. The government was reorganized, and after a national, freely contested election, the Transitional National Assembly, which chose Isaias as President of the PGE, was expanded to include both EPLF and non-EPLF members. The EPLF established itself as a political party, the People's Front for Democracy and Justice (PFDJ). The PGE declared that during a 4-year transition period it would draft and ratify a constitution, draft a law on political parties, draft a press law, and carry out elections for a constitutional government.

In March 1994, the PGE created a constitutional commission charged with drafting a constitution flexible enough to meet the current needs of a population suffering from 30 years of civil war as well as those of the future, when prospective stability and prosperity would change the political landscape. Commission members traveled throughout the country and to Eritrean communities abroad holding meetings to explain constitutional options to the people and to solicit their input. A new constitution was ratified in 1997 but has not been implemented, and general elections have not been held. The government had announced that Transitional National Assembly elections would take place in December 2001, but those were postponed and new elections have not been rescheduled.

The present government structure includes legislative, executive, and judicial bodies. The legislature, the Transitional National Assembly, comprises 75 members of the PFDJ and 75 additional popularly elected members. The Transitional National Assembly is the highest legal power in the government until the establishment of a democratic, constitutional government. The legislature sets the internal and external policies of the government, regulates implementation of those policies, approves the budget, and elects the president of the country. The president nominates individuals to head the various ministries, authorities, commissions, and offices, and the Transitional National Assembly ratifies those nominations. The cabinet is the country's executive branch. It is composed of 17 ministers and chaired by the president. It implements policies, regulations, and laws and is accountable to the Transitional National Assembly. The ministries are agriculture; defense; education; energy and mines; finance; fisheries; foreign affairs; health; information; labor and human welfare; land, water, and environment; local governments; justice; public works; trade and industry; transportation and communication; and tourism.

Nominally, the judiciary operates independently of both the legislative and executive bodies, with a court system that extends from the village through to the district, provincial, and national levels. In practice, however, the independence of the judiciary is limited. In 2001, for example, the president of the High Court was detained after criticizing the government for judicial interference.

In September 2001, after several months in which a number of prominent PFDJ party members had publicly aired grievances against the government and in which they called for implementation of the constitution and the holding of elections, the government instituted a crackdown. Eleven prominent dissidents, members of what had come to be known as the Group of 15, were arrested and held without charge in an unknown location. At the same time, the government shut down the independent press and arrested its reporters and editors, holding them incommunicado and without charge. In subsequent weeks, the government arrested other individuals, including two Eritrean employees of the U.S. Embassy.

PRINCIPAL GOVERNMENT OFFICIALS

President of the State of Eritrea and Chairman of the Executive Council of the PFDJ--Isaias Afwerki

Director, Office of the President--Yemane Ghebremeskel
Minister of Defense--Sebhat Ephrem
Minister of Foreign Affairs--Osman Saleh
Minister of Finance--Berhane Abrehe
Charge d'Affaires to the United States--Berhane Gebrehiwet

Eritrea maintains an embassy in the United States at 1708 New Hampshire Ave., NW, Washington, DC 20009 (tel. 202-319-1991).

Economy

Agriculture contributed 24% to GDP as of 2007, and it employed about 17% of the work force in 2009. Agricultural exports include cotton, fruits and vegetables, hides, and meat, but farmers are largely dependent on rain-fed agriculture, and growth in this and other sectors is hampered by lack of a dependable water supply. Worker remittances and other private transfers from abroad contribute about 32% of GDP.

While in the past the Government of Eritrea stated that it was committed to a market economy and privatization, the government and the ruling PFDJ party maintain complete control of the economy. The government has imposed an arbitrary and complex set of regulatory requirements that discourage investment from both foreign and domestic sources, and it often reclaims successful private enterprises and property.

After independence, Eritrea had established a growing and healthy economy. But the 1998-2000 war with Ethiopia had a major negative impact on the economy and discouraged investment. Eritrea lost many valuable economic assets during the last round of fighting in May-June 2000, when a significant portion of its territory in the agriculturally important west and south was occupied by Ethiopia. During this period, more than one million Eritreans were displaced, although nearly all had been resettled by 2007. According to World Bank estimates, Eritreans also lost livestock worth some $225 million, and 55,000 homes worth $41 million during the war. Damage to public buildings, including hospitals, was estimated at $24 million. Much of the transportation and communication infrastructure is outmoded and deteriorating, although a large volume of intercity road-building activity is currently underway. The government sought international assistance for various development projects and mobilized young Eritreans serving in the national service to repair crumbling roads and dams. In 2005, the government asked the U.S. Agency for International Development (USAID) to cease operations in Eritrea.

According to the International Monetary Fund (IMF), post-border war recovery was impaired by 4 consecutive years of recurrent drought that have reduced the already low domestic food production capacity. The government reports that harvests have improved but provides no data to support these claims. Eritrea currently suffers from large structural fiscal deficits caused by high levels of spending on defense, which have resulted in the stock of debt rising to unsustainable levels. Exports have collapsed due to strict controls on foreign currencies and trade, as well as a closed border with Ethiopia, which was the major trading partner for Eritrea prior to the war. In 2006, Eritrea normalized relations with Sudan and began to open the border to trade between the two countries. Large and persistent transfers from Eritreans living abroad offer significant support to the economy.

The port in Massawa has been rehabilitated and is being developed. In addition, the government has begun to export fish and sea cucumbers from the Red Sea to markets in Europe and Asia on a limited basis. A newly constructed airport in Massawa capable of handling jets could facilitate the export of high-value perishable seafood.

Defense

During the war for independence, the EPLF fighting force grew to almost 110,000 fighters, about 3% of the total population of Eritrea. In 1993, Eritrea embarked on a phased program to demobilize 50%-60% of the army, which had by then shrunk to about 95,000. During the first phase of demobilization in 1993, some 26,000 soldiers--most of who enlisted after 1990--were demobilized. The second phase of demobilization, which occurred the following year, demobilized more than 17,000 soldiers who had joined the EPLF before 1990 and in many cases had seen considerable combat experience. Many of these fighters had spent their entire adult lives in the EPLF and lacked the social, personal, and vocational skills to become competitive in the work place. As a result, they received higher compensation, more intensive training, and more psychological counseling than the first group. Special attention was given to women fighters, who made up some 30% of the EPLF's combat troops. By 1998, the army had shrunk to 47,000.

The moves to demobilize were abruptly reversed after the outbreak of the 1998-2000 war with Ethiopia over the contested border. During the war, which is estimated to have resulted in well over 100,000 casualties on the two sides, Eritrea's armed forces expanded to close to 300,000 members, almost 10% of the population. This imposed a huge economic burden on the country. The war ended with a cessation of hostilities agreement in June 2000, followed by a peace agreement signed in December of the same year. The International Monetary Fund (IMF) estimates that the economy shrank by more than 8% in 2000, although it rebounded somewhat in 2001.

The government has been slow to demobilize its military after the end of the conflict, although it formulated an ambitious demobilization plan with the participation of the World Bank. A pilot demobilization program involving 5,000 soldiers began in November 2001 and was to be followed immediately thereafter by a first phase in which some 65,000 soldiers would be demobilized. This was delayed repeatedly. In 2003, the government began to demobilize some of those slated for the first phase; however, the government maintains a "national service" program, which includes most of the male population between 18-40 and the female population between 18-27. The program essentially serves as a reserve force and can be mobilized quickly. There are estimates that one in twenty Eritreans actively serve in the military.

Presently, the U.S. has no military-to-military cooperation with Eritrea.

FOREIGN RELATIONS

Eritrea is a member of the Common Market of Eastern and Southern Africa (COMESA) and the African Union (AU). Eritrea maintains diplomatic relations with the United States, Italy, and several other European nations, including the United Kingdom, Germany, Norway, and the Netherlands. Relations with these countries became strained as a result of the 2001 government crackdown against political dissidents and others, the closure of the independent press, and limits on civil liberties.

Eritrea's relations with its neighbors are strained. Eritrea and Djibouti had a military confrontation in June 2008 along their border. In January 2009, the UN Security Council adopted a resolution calling for Eritrea to withdraw to positions of the status quo ante, acknowledge its border dispute with Djibouti, engage actively in dialogue to defuse the tension, and engage in diplomatic efforts leading to a mutually acceptable settlement of the border issue. Although a territorial dispute with Yemen over the Haynish Islands was settled by international arbitration, tensions over traditional fishing rights with Yemen resurfaced in 2002. The relationship to date remains cordial. Relations with

Sudan were colored by occasional incidents involving the extremist group Eritrean Islamic Jihad (EIJ)--believed by the Eritrean Government to be supported by the National Islamic Front government in Khartoum--and by Eritrean support for the Sudanese opposition coalition, the National Democratic Alliance. Eritrea normalized relations with Sudan in 2006.

Eritrea-Ethiopia Border Dispute

Following the 1998-2000 war, a UN peacekeeping mission, the UN Mission in Ethiopia and Eritrea (UNMEE), was established and monitored a 25-kilometer-wide Temporary Security Zone separating the two sides. Eritrean restrictions on UNMEE led to its termination in July 2008.

Per the terms of the cessation of hostilities agreement, two commissions were established: one to delimit and demarcate the border and the other to weigh compensation claims by both sides. The Eritrea-Ethiopia Boundary Commission (EEBC) announced its decision in April 2002. Demarcation was expected to begin in 2003, but did not progress due to disagreements between the parties. The EEBC announced a demarcation decision effective November 2007. Eritrea accepted the decision, but Ethiopia rejected it. The situation remains at an impasse.

In August 2009, the Eritrea-Ethiopia Claims Commission (EECC) delivered its final awards regarding international law violations during the 1998-2000 border war. The Claims Commission awarded Eritrea $161 million for damages caused by Ethiopia with an additional $2 million for individual claims. Ethiopia was awarded $174 million for damages caused by Eritrea. Eritrea cited interference which impaired the administration of justice and challenged the plausibility of evidence but announced it accepts the award of the Claims Commission without equivocation.

U.S.-ERITREAN RELATIONS

The U.S. consulate in Asmara was first established in 1942. In 1953, the United States signed a mutual defense treaty with Ethiopia. The treaty granted the United States control and expansion of the important British military communications base at Kagnew near Asmara. In the 1960s, as many as 4,000 U.S. military personnel were stationed at Kagnew. In the 1970s, technological advances in the satellite and communications fields made the communications station at Kagnew increasingly obsolete. In 1974, Kagnew Station drastically reduced its personnel complement. In early 1977, the United States informed the Ethiopian Government that it intended to close Kagnew Station permanently by September 30, 1977. In the meantime, U.S. relations with the Mengistu regime were worsening. In April 1977, Mengistu abrogated the 1953 mutual defense treaty and ordered a reduction of U.S. personnel in Ethiopia, including the closure of Kagnew Communications Center and the consulate in Asmara. In August 1992, the United States reopened its consulate in Asmara, staffed with one officer. On April 27, 1993, the United States recognized Eritrea as an independent state, and on June 11, diplomatic relations were established, with a charge d'affaires. The first U.S. Ambassador arrived later that year.

In the past, the United States has provided substantial assistance to Eritrea, including food and development. In FY 2004, the United States provided over $65 million in humanitarian aid to Eritrea, including $58.1 million in food assistance and $3.47 million in refugee support. In 2005, the Government of Eritrea told USAID to cease operations. At the Eritrean Government's request, the United States no longer provides bilateral development assistance to Eritrea.

U.S. interests in Eritrea include encouraging Eritrea to contribute to regional stability, consolidating the peace with Ethiopia and Djibouti, encouraging progress toward establishing a democratic political culture, supporting Eritrean efforts to become constructively involved in solving regional problems, assisting Eritrea in dealing with its humanitarian and development needs, and promoting economic reform.

In: Humanitarian Crisis and Response ...   ISBN: 978-1-61942-540-8
Editors: C.J. Newsome and H.I. Herron © 2012 Nova Science Publishers, Inc.

Chapter 13

DJIBOUTI COUNTRY PROFILE

United States Department of State

Official Name: Republic of Djibouti

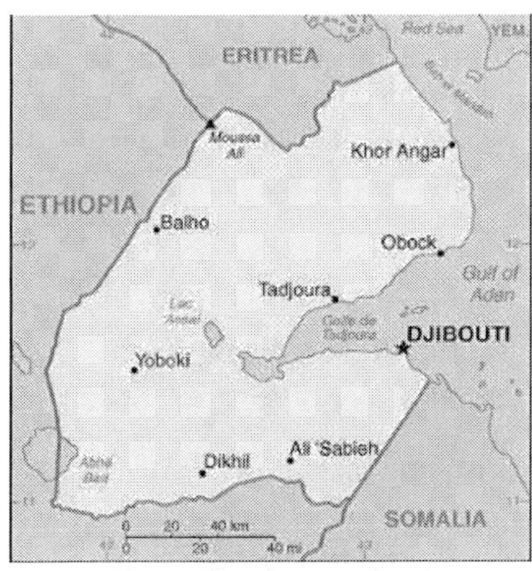

Flag of Djibouti.

GEOGRAPHY

Area: 23,180 sq. km; slightly smaller than Massachusetts.
Cities: *Capital*--Djibouti. *Other cities*--Dikhil, Arta, Ali-Sabieh, Obock, Tadjourah.
Terrain: Coastal desert.
Climate: Torrid and dry.

PEOPLE

Nationality: *Noun and adjective*--Djiboutian(s).
Population (2011 est.): 757,074.
Annual population growth rate (2011 est.): 2.237%.
Ethnic groups: Somali, Afar, Ethiopian, Arab, French, and Italian.
Religions: Muslim 94%, Christian 6%.
Languages: French and Arabic (official); Somali and Afar widely used.
Education: *Literacy*--67.9%.
Health: Infant mortality rate--54.94/1,000. Life expectancy--61 years.
Work force: Low employment rate. The largest employers are the Government of Djibouti, including telecommunications and electricity; Port of Djibouti; and airport. The U.S. Government, including the U.S. military base at Camp Lemonnier, is also a large employer. Able-bodied unemployed population (est. 2007)--59%.

GOVERNMENT

Type: Republic.
Constitution: Ratified September 1992 by referendum.
Independence: June 27, 1977.
Branches: *Executive*--president. *Legislative*--65-member parliament, cabinet, prime minister. *Judicial*--based on French civil law system, traditional practices, and Islamic law.
Administrative subdivisions: 6 regions (districts)--Ali-Sabieh, Arta, Dikhil, Djibouti City, Obock, and Tadjourah.
Political parties: People's Rally for Progress (RPP); National Democratic Party (PND); Front for the Restoration of Unity and Democracy (FRUD);

Djibouti Development Party (PDD); People's Social Democratic Party (PPSD); Republican Alliance for Democracy (ARD); Union for Democracy and Justice (UDJ); Union of Reform Partisans (UPR).

Suffrage: Universal at 18.

National holiday: Independence Day, June 27.

ECONOMY

GDP (2010 est.): $1.14 billion.

Per capita income (2010 est.): $2,800.

Natural resources: Minerals (salt, perlite, gold, gypsum, limestone) and energy resources (geothermal, wind, and solar).

Agriculture (less than 3% of GDP): *Products*--livestock, fishing, and limited commercial crops, including fruits and vegetables.

Industry: *Types*--banking and insurance (12.5% of GDP), public administration (22% of GDP), construction and public works, manufacturing, commerce, and agriculture.

Trade (2006 est.): *Imports*--$1.555 billion: consists of basic commodities, including food and beverages, pharmaceutical drugs, transport equipment, chemicals, and petroleum products. *Exports*--$340 million: re-exports, hides and skins, and coffee (in-transit). *Major markets* (2004)--France, Ethiopia, Somalia, India, China, and Saudi Arabia and other Arabian peninsula countries.

People

About two-thirds of the Republic of Djibouti's inhabitants live in the capital city. The indigenous population is divided between the majority Somalis (predominantly of the Issa tribe, with minority Issaq and Gadabursi representation) and the Afars (Danakils). All are Cushitic-speaking peoples, and nearly all are Muslim. Among the 15,000 foreigners residing in Djibouti, the French are the most numerous. Among the French are approximately 3,000 troops.

History

The Republic of Djibouti gained its independence on June 27, 1977. It is the successor to French Somaliland (later called the French Territory of the Afars and Issas), which was created in the first half of the 19th century as a result of French interest in the Horn of Africa. However, the history of Djibouti, recorded in poetry and songs of its nomadic peoples, goes back thousands of years to a time when Djiboutians traded hides and skins for the perfumes and spices of ancient Egypt, India, and China. Through close contacts with the Arabian Peninsula for more than 1,000 years, the Somali and Afar tribes in this region became the first on the African continent to adopt Islam.

It was Rochet d'Hericourt's exploration into Shoa (1839-42) that marked the beginning of French interest in the African shores of the Red Sea. Further exploration by Henri Lambert, French Consular Agent at Aden, and Captain Fleuriot de Langle led to a treaty of friendship and assistance between France and the sultans of Raheita, Tadjourah, and Gobaad, from whom the French purchased the anchorage of Obock (1862).

Growing French interest in the area took place against a backdrop of British activity in Egypt and the opening of the Suez Canal in 1869. In 1884-85, France expanded its protectorate to include the shores of the Gulf of Tadjourah and Somaliland. Boundaries of the protectorate, marked out in 1897 by France and Emperor Menelik II of Ethiopia, were affirmed further by agreements with Ethiopian Emperor Haile Selassie I in 1945 and 1954.

The administrative capital was moved from Obock to Djibouti in 1892. In 1896, Djibouti was named French Somaliland. Djibouti, which has a good natural harbor and ready access to the Ethiopian highlands, attracted trade caravans crossing East Africa as well as Somali settlers from the south. The Franco-Ethiopian railway, linking Djibouti to the heart of Ethiopia, was begun in 1897 and reached Addis Ababa in June 1917, further facilitating the increase of trade.

During the Italian invasion and occupation of Ethiopia in the 1930s and during World War II, constant border skirmishes occurred between French and Italian forces. The area was ruled by the Vichy (French) government from the fall of France until December 1942, and fell under British blockade during that period. Free French and the Allied forces recaptured Djibouti at the end of 1942. A local battalion from Djibouti participated in the liberation of France in 1944.

On July 22, 1957, the colony was reorganized to give the people considerable self-government. On the same day, a decree applying the Overseas Reform Act (Loi Cadre) of June 23, 1956, established a territorial assembly that elected eight of its members to an executive council. Members of the executive council were responsible for one or more of the territorial services and carried the title of minister. The council advised the French-appointed governor general.

In a September 1958 constitutional referendum, French Somaliland opted to join the French community as an overseas territory. This act entitled the region to representation by one deputy and one senator in the French Parliament, and one counselor in the French Union Assembly.

The first elections to the territorial assembly were held on November 23, 1958, under a system of proportional representation. In the next assembly elections (1963), a new electoral law was enacted. Representation was abolished in exchange for a system of straight plurality vote based on lists submitted by political parties in seven designated districts. Ali Aref Bourhan, allegedly of Turkish origin, was selected to be the president of the executive council. French President Charles de Gaulle's August 1966 visit to Djibouti was marked by 2 days of public demonstrations by Somalis demanding independence. On September 21, 1966, Louis Saget, appointed governor general of the territory after the demonstrations, announced the French Government's decision to hold a referendum to determine whether the people would remain within the French Republic or become independent. In March 1967, 60% chose to continue the territory's association with France.

In July of that year, a directive from Paris formally changed the name of the region to the French Territory of Afars and Issas. The directive also reorganized the governmental structure of the territory, making the senior French representative (formerly the governor general) a high commissioner. In addition, the executive council was redesignated as the council of government, with nine members.

In 1975, the French Government began to accommodate increasingly insistent demands for independence. In June 1976, the territory's citizenship law, which favored the Afar minority, was revised to reflect more closely the weight of the Issa Somali. The electorate voted for independence in a May 1977 referendum. The Republic of Djibouti was established on June 27, 1977, and Hassan Gouled Aptidon became the country's first president. In 1981, he was again elected president of Djibouti. He was re-elected, unopposed, to a second 6-year term in April 1987 and to a third 6-year term in May 1993 multiparty elections.

In early 1992, the constitution permitted the legalization of four political parties for a period of 10 years, after which a complete multiparty system would be installed. By the time of the December 1992 national assembly elections, only three had qualified. They were the Rassemblement Populaire Pour le Progres (People's Rally for Progress--RPP), which was the only legal party from 1981 until 1992; the Parti du Renouveau Democratique (The Party for Democratic Renewal--PRD); and the Parti National Democratique (National Democratic Party--PND). Only the RPP and the PRD contested the national assembly elections, and the PND withdrew, claiming that there were too many unanswered questions on the conduct of the elections and too many opportunities for government fraud. The RPP won all 65 seats in the national assembly, with a turnout of less than 50% of the electorate.

In early November 1991, civil war erupted in Djibouti between the government and a predominantly Afar rebel group, the Front for the Restoration of Unity and Democracy (FRUD). The FRUD signed a peace accord with the government in December 1994, ending the conflict. Two FRUD members were made cabinet members, and in the presidential elections of 1999 the FRUD campaigned in support of the RPP.

In 1999, Ismail Omar Guelleh--President Hassan Gouled Aptidon's chief of staff, head of security, and key adviser for over 20 years--was elected to the presidency as the RPP candidate. He received 74% of the vote, with the other 26% going to opposition candidate Moussa Ahmed Idriss of the Unified Djiboutian Opposition (ODU). For the first time since independence, no group boycotted the election. Moussa Ahmed Idriss and the ODU later challenged the results based on election "irregularities" and the assertion that "foreigners" had voted in various districts of the capital; however, international and locally based observers considered the election to be generally fair, and cited only minor technical difficulties. Guelleh took the oath of office as the second President of the Republic of Djibouti on May 8, 1999, with the support of an alliance between the RPP and the government-recognized section of the Afar-led FRUD.

In February 2000, another branch of FRUD signed a peace accord with the government. On May 12, 2001, President Guelleh presided over the signing of what was termed the final peace accord officially ending the decade-long civil war between the government and the armed faction of the FRUD. The peace accord successfully completed the peace process begun on February 7, 2000 in Paris. Ahmed Dini Ahmed represented the FRUD.

Government and Political Conditions

Djibouti is a republic whose electorate approved the current constitution in September 1992. Many laws and decrees from before independence remain in effect.

In April 2011, President Ismail Omar Guelleh was re-elected for a third term. In April 2005, Guelleh had been re-elected at the head of a five-party coalition that included the FRUD and other parties. A loose coalition of opposition parties boycotted the 2005 election. Currently, political power is shared by a Somali Issa president and an Afar prime minister, with an Afar career diplomat as Foreign Minister and other cabinet posts roughly divided. However, some Djiboutians feel that Somali Issas are likely overrepresented in the government, civil service, and ruling party. That, together with a shortage of non-government employment, has bred resentment and continued political competition between the Somali Issas and the Afars. In March 2006, Djibouti held its first regional elections and began implementing a decentralization plan. Parliamentary elections were held in February 2008. The broad pro-government coalition, including FRUD candidates, again ran unopposed when the government refused to meet opposition preconditions for participation.

Djibouti has its own armed forces, including a small army, which grew significantly with the start of the civil war in 1991. With the 2001 final peace accord between the government and the Afar-dominated FRUD, the armed forces have been downsized. The country's security is supplemented by a formal security accord with the Government of France, which guarantees Djibouti's territorial integrity against foreign incursions. France maintains one of its largest military bases outside France in Djibouti. There are some 3,000 French troops stationed in Djibouti, including units of the famed French Foreign Legion.

The right to own property is respected in Djibouti. The government has reorganized the labor unions. While there have been open elections of union leaders in the past, some labor leaders allege interference in their internal elections. Others voice opposition to newly-implemented labor laws that apply to new jobs created in free zones and that are less favorable to labor.

In 2002, following a broad national debate, Djibouti enacted a new "Family Law" enhancing the protection of women and children, unifying legal treatment of all women, and replacing Sharia. The government established a minister for women's affairs and is engaged in an ongoing effort to increase public recognition of women's rights and to ensure enforcement. The government is leading efforts to stop illegal and abusive traditional practices, including female genital mutilation. As the result of an ongoing effort, the percentage of girls attending primary school increased significantly and is now more than 50%. However, women's rights and family planning continue to face difficult challenges, many stemming from acute poverty in both rural and urban areas. With female ministers and members of parliament, the presence of women in government has increased. Despite the gains, education of girls still lags behind boys, and employment opportunities are better for male applicants.

PRINCIPAL GOVERNMENT OFFICIALS

President--Ismail Omar Guelleh
Prime Minister--Dileita Mohamed Dileita
Foreign Affairs--Mahamoud Ali Youssouf
Ambassador to the United Nations and the United States--Roble Olhaye Oudine

Djibouti's mission to the UN is located at 866 UN Plaza, Suite 4011, New York, NY 10017 (tel. 212-753-3163). Djibouti's embassy in Washington is located at Suite 515, 1156 15th Street, NW, Washington, DC 20005 (tel. 202-331-0270; fax 202-331-0302).

Economy

Djibouti's economy depends largely on its proximity to the large Ethiopian market and a large foreign expatriate community. Its main economic activities are the Port of Djibouti, the banking sector, the airport, and the operation of the Addis Ababa-Djibouti railroad. During the "lost decade" following the brunt of its civil war (1991-94), there was a significant diversion of government budgetary resources from developmental and social services to military needs. However, from 2001 on, Djibouti has become a magnet for private sector capital investment, attracting foreign direct investment inflows that now top $200 million annually. It has also significantly improved its finances, paying current salaries, maintaining reserves, and generating a growth rate in 2008 of approximately 5.8%. Djibouti has become a significant regional banking hub, with approximately $600 million in dollar deposits. Its currency, the Djiboutian franc, was linked to the dollar (and to gold) in 1949 and appreciated twice over the interim when the dollar was devalued and then freed to float. Agriculture and industry are little developed, in part due to the harsh climate, high production costs, unskilled labor, and limited natural resources. Mineral deposits exist in the country, but with the exception of an extraordinary salt deposit at Lac Assal, the lowest point in Africa, they have not been exploited. The arid soil is unproductive--89% is desert wasteland, 10% is pasture, and 1% is forested. Deforestation for charcoal is a significant problem, as it now replaces expensive imported cooking gas in many urban homes. Services and commerce provide most of the gross domestic product.

Djibouti's most important economic asset is its strategic location on the busy shipping route between the Mediterranean Sea and the Indian Ocean. Roughly 60% of all commercial ships in the world use its waters from the Red Sea through the Bab-el-Mandeb strait and into the Gulf of Aden and the Indian Ocean. Its port is an increasingly important transshipment point for containers as well as a destination port for Ethiopian trade. In 2009, Djibouti and Dubai Ports World inaugurated the state-of-the-art, $300 million Doraleh Container Terminal. The older portion of the port will continue serving as a general shipping, bulk cargo, and break-bulk facility and also as the host of a small French naval facility.

Business soared at the Port of Djibouti when hostilities between Eritrea and Ethiopia denied Ethiopia access to the Eritrean Port of Assab. Djibouti became the only significant port for landlocked Ethiopia, handling all its imports and exports, including huge shipments of U.S. food aid in 2000 during the drought and famine. In 2000, Dubai Ports World took over management of Djibouti's port and later its customs and airport operations. The result has been a significant increase in investment, efficiency, activity, and port revenues. The Addis Ababa-Djibouti railroad is the only line serving central and southeastern Ethiopia. The single-track railway needs upgrades, but remains an important source of employment. A weekly train from Ethiopia brings in most of Djibouti's fresh fruits and vegetables. The bulk of Ethiopia-bound imports from Djibouti's port are transported via truck. Principal exports from the region transiting Djibouti are coffee, salt, live animals, hides, dried beans, cereals, other agricultural products, and wax. Djibouti itself has few exports, and the majority of its imports come from France. Most imports are consumed in Djibouti, and the remainder go to Ethiopia and northwestern Somalia. Djibouti's unfavorable balance of trade is offset partially by invisible earnings such as transit taxes and harbor dues. In 2007, U.S. exports to Djibouti totaled $59 million, while U.S. imports from Djibouti were about $4 million.

The city of Djibouti has the only paved airport in the republic. Djibouti has one of the most liberal economic regimes in Africa, with almost unrestricted banking and commerce sectors.

FOREIGN RELATIONS

Military and economic agreements with France provide continued security and economic assistance. Djibouti serves as the headquarters for the European Union's "Atalanta" naval task force and for a Japanese contingent, combating piracy off the coast of Somalia. Djibouti is a member of the League of Arab States (LAS) and the Organization of the Islamic Conference (OIC), as well as the African Union (AU), the Intergovernmental Authority on Development (IGAD), the Common Market for Eastern and Southern Africa (COMESA), and the International Organization of Francophones ("Organisation international de la Francophonie," or OIF). Djibouti is also a member of the East African Standby Brigade Coordination Mechanism (EASBRICOM), which is currently commanded by a Djiboutian general.

Djibouti is greatly affected by events in Somalia and Ethiopia, so relations are important and, at times, delicate. The 1991 falls of the Siad Barre and Mengistu governments in Somalia and Ethiopia, respectively, caused Djibouti to face national security threats due to instability in the neighboring states and a massive influx of refugees estimated at 100,000 from Somalia and Ethiopia. In 2000, after 3 years of insufficient rain, 50,000 drought victims entered Djibouti. The number of refugees in Djibouti doubled from 2006 to late 2009, with approximately 12,000 registered with the UN High Commissioner for Refugees (UNHCR), predominantly from Somalia and Ethiopia. As of fall 2011, UNHCR reported 18,000 registered Somali refugees in Djibouti.

In 1996, a revitalized organization of seven East African states, IGAD, established its secretariat in Djibouti. IGAD's mandate is for regional cooperation and economic integration, and it has also sought to play a positive role promoting regional stability, including its efforts in support of Somalia's Transitional Federal Government (TFG).

Djibouti seeks to play a stabilizing role in the frequently tense regional politics of the Horn of Africa. Djibouti hosted UN-sponsored Somali reconciliation talks in 2008-2009 (the "Djibouti Process"), and provided military training for TFG troops in late 2009. Djibouti became Ethiopia's sole link to the sea when fighting broke out between Ethiopia and Eritrea in 1998.

Djibouti's relations with Eritrea have become strained after a military confrontation in June 2008 along their shared border.

Djibouti continues to cultivate cordial relations with Ethiopia, reflecting the fundamental economic ties between the two countries and a long tradition of interchanges. However, rising tensions in Somalia and Ethiopian military involvement in Somalia in 2007 fueled widespread criticism of Ethiopia among Djibouti's majority Somali-speaking population. President Guelleh attended the 2007 Africa Union summit in Ethiopia and supports the African Union peacekeeping operation for Somalia (AMISOM).

U.S.-DJIBOUTIAN RELATIONS

In April 1977, the United States established a Consulate General in Djibouti and upon independence in June 1977 raised the status of its mission to an embassy. The first U.S. Ambassador to the Republic of Djibouti arrived in October 1980. Over the past decade, the United States has been a principal provider of humanitarian assistance for famine relief, and has sponsored health care, education, good governance, and security assistance programs.

Djibouti is a U.S. partner on security, regional stability, and humanitarian efforts in the Horn of Africa. The Djiboutian Government has been very supportive of U.S. and Western interests, particularly since the Gulf crisis of 1990-91 and after the terrorist attacks of September 11, 2001. President Guelleh continues to take a very proactive position against terrorism. In 2002, Djibouti agreed to host a U.S. military presence at Camp Lemonnier, a former French Foreign Legion base outside the capital that now houses approximately 2,200 American personnel. U.S. service members have been instrumental in providing humanitarian, development, and security assistance to the people and governments of the Horn of Africa and Yemen. Djibouti has also allowed the U.S. military, as well as other nations, access to its port and airport facilities.

The U.S. Agency for International Development's (USAID) Food for Peace program maintains a warehouse for pre-positioned emergency food relief in Djibouti--the only one of its kind outside the continental United States--allowing expedient delivery of humanitarian assistance to famine-stricken countries from Africa to Asia. International Broadcasting Bureau (IBB) facilities in Djibouti transmit Arabic-language Radio Sawa programming and Voice of America (VOA) Somali Service broadcasts to neighboring Somalia and the Arabian Peninsula.

CHAPTER SOURCES

The following chapters have been previously published:

Chapter 1 - This is an edited, reformatted and augmented version of a Congressional Research Service publication, CRS Report for Congress R42046, from www.crs.gov, dated September 30, 2011.

Chapter 2 - These remarks were delivered as testimony given by Nancy E. Lindborg, Assistant Administrator, Bureau for Democracy, Conflict, and Humanitarian Assistance, U.S. Agency for International Development, before the Committee on Foreign Relations, Subcommittee on African Affairs, United States Senate, Drought and Famine in the Horn of Africa, on August 4, 2011.

Chapter 3 - These remarks were delivered as testimony given by Principal Deputy Assistant Secretary Don Yamamoto, Bureau of African Affairs, U.S. Department of State, before the Senate Foreign Relations, Subcommittee on African Affairs, "Responding to Drought and Famine in the Horn of Africa", on Wednesday, August, 3, 2011.

Chapter 4 - These remarks were delivered as testimony given by Testimony of Reuben E. Brigety, II, Deputy Assistant Secretary, Bureau for Population, Refugees, and Migration, U.S. Department of State, before the Committee on Foreign Relations, Subcommittee on African Affairs, United States Senate, Drought and Famine in the Horn of Africa, on August 3, 2011.

Chapter 5 - These remarks were delivered as statement given by Jeremy Konyndyk, Director of Policy and Advocacy, Mercy Corps, U.S. Senate Committee on Foreign Relations, Subcommittee on Africa, Hearing on: *Responding to Drought and Famine in the Horn of Africa, on* August 3, 2011.

Chapter 6 - These remarks were delivered as testimony given on August 3, 2011. Dr. J. Peter Pham, Director, Michael S. Ansari Africa Center, Atlantic Council before the United States Senate Committee on Foreign Relations, Subcommittee on African Affairs.

Chapter 7 - These remarks were delivered as testimony given on September 8, 2011. Katherine L. Zimmerman, Critical Threats Project Analyst, American Enterprise Institute, American Enterprise Institute for Public Policy Research before the House Committee on Foreign Affairs, Subcommittee on Africa, Global Health, and Human Rights.

Chapter 8 - These remarks were delivered as testimony given on September 8, 2011. Shannon Scribner, Humanitarian Policy Manager, Oxfam America before the House Committee on Foreign Affairs, Subcommittee on Africa, Global Health, and Human Rights.

Chapter 9 - The website information has been edited, reformatted and augmented from, www.state.gov/r/pa/ei/bgn/2863.htm.

Chapter 10 - The website information has been edited, reformatted and augmented from, www.state.gov/r/pa/ei/bgn/2962.htm.

Chapter 11 - The website information has been edited, reformatted and augmented from, www.state.gov/r/pa/ei/bgn/2859.htm.

Chapter 12 - The website information has been edited, reformatted and augmented from, www.state.gov/r/pa/ei/bgn/2854.htm.

Chapter 13 - The website information has been edited, reformatted and augmented from, www.state.gov/r/pa/ei/bgn/5482.htm.

C

E

J

K

L

M